# British Railways
# The First 25 Years

## Volume 11
## North Wales, Chester and the Wirral

'Royal Scot' 4-6-0 No. 46125 *3rd Carabinier* leaves the Conway tubular bridge with a Down express on 8th June 1956. Originally named *Lancashire Witch* after the 0-4-0 built in 1828 by Robert Stephenson & Company, it was converted from parallel to taper boiler in August 1943 and was allocated to Crewe North from March 1954 until May 1962. *John Head/Rail Archive Stephenson*

# BRITISH RAILWAYS

## The First 25 Years

### Volume 11
### North Wales, Chester and the Wirral

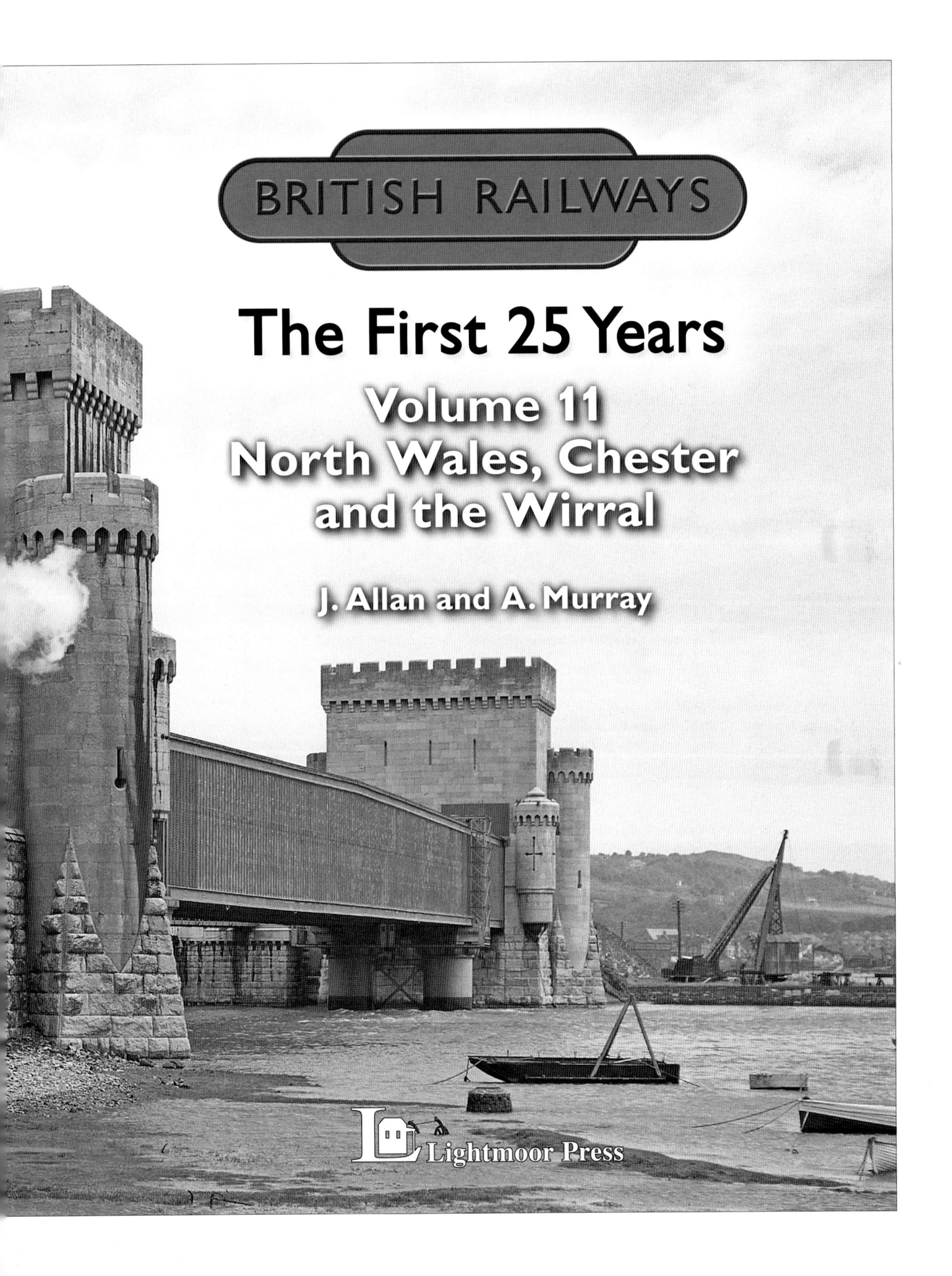

J. Allan and A. Murray

Lightmoor Press

All ten of the former Crosti boiler 2-10-0s were transferred to Birkenhead Mollington Street during the mid-1960s. No. 92026 had arrived from Newton Heath in May 1965 and has the 8H shed code crudely chalked on its smokebox. By August 1965 over fifty 2-10-0s were allocated to the shed and were particularly associated with the heavy iron ore trains which ran between Bidston Docks and the John Summers steelworks at Shotton on the northern side of the River Dee.

*Cover photographs*

*Front upper*: Double chimney 'Castle' No. 7014 *Caerhays Castle* departs from Chester General in the early 1960s. It was allocated to Old Oak Common from August 1961 until June 1962 when it moved to Wolverhampton Stafford Road.

*Front lower*: 'Royal Scot' 4-6-0 No. 46147 *The Northamptonshire Regiment* passes Aber with the Down 'Irish Mail' on 3rd September 1957. It went back and forth between Longsight and Holyhead from September 1955 until October 1957 and was at the Anglesey shed but officially on loan at the date of this picture. This train often had a former GWR 'Siphon G' at the front carrying mail and parcels.
K. L. Cook/Rail Archive Stephenson

*Back upper*: GCR Robinson 'C14' 4-4-2T No. 67442 at Seacombe with a train to Wrexham on 9th April 1955. The 'C14' class was a development of the more common 'C13' 4-4-2T which were the mainstay of the Great Central passenger services on the Wirral for half a century. No. 67442 was built by Beyer, Peacock & Co. Ltd in 1907 and was allocated to Wrexham Rhosddu from July 1948 until withdrawn in November 1957.

*Back centre*: Two of the BR-built three-car electrical multiple units with Motor Brake Second No. M 28689 M at the front wait to leave Rock Ferry for Liverpool Central on 23rd July 1967. The nineteen three-car Wirral units were designed by Stanier for the LM&SR in the late-1930s and were significantly ahead of their time. They employed all-welded, stressed alloy construction and had driving coaches with modern rounded front ends. The interiors were open saloons and each coach had double-leaf air-operated sliding doors.

*Back lower*: A Derby 'Lightweight' DMU arrives at Betws-y-Coed on a service from Blaenau Ffestiniog to Llandudno in the early 1960s. Diesel multiple units had been introduced on the Conway Valley line in 1956 and were very successful in attracting more passengers.

© Lightmoor Press, J. Allan, A. Murray, 2021.
Designed by Stephen Phillips.

British Library Cataloguing-in-Publication Data.
A catalogue record for this book is available from the British Library.
ISBN 978-1-911038-85-6

All rights reserved. No part of this publication may be reproduced, stored in a retrieval system or transmitted in any form or by any means, electronic, mechanical, photocopying, recording or otherwise, without the written permission of the publisher.

**LIGHTMOOR PRESS**
**Unit 144B, Lydney Trading Estate, Harbour Road,**
**Lydney, Gloucestershire GL15 4EJ**
**www.lightmoor.co.uk**

Lightmoor Press is an imprint of
Black Dwarf Lightmoor Publications Ltd.

Printed in Poland
www.lfbookservices.co.uk

# Contents

| | |
|---|---|
| **Introduction and Acknowledgements** | 7 |
| | |
| **1 Gobowen to Chester** | **8** |
| Park Hall Halt | 8 |
| Gobowen | 9 |
| Cefn Dee Viaduct | 13 |
| Ruabon | 13 |
| Wrexham Croes Newydd | 17 |
| Croes Newydd shed | 19 |
| Wrexham General | 21 |
| Gresford | 21 |
| Saltney | 23 |
| | |
| **2 Wrexham to the Wirral** | **25** |
| Wrexham | 25 |
| Wrexham Central | 25 |
| Wrexham Exchange | 27 |
| Rhosddu shed | 28 |
| Buckley Junction | 29 |
| Hawarden | 30 |
| Shotton High Level | 30 |
| Hawarden Bridge | 32 |
| Sealand | 33 |
| Bidston | 34 |
| Bidston shed | 36 |
| Seacombe | 38 |
| | |
| **3 The Wirral electrics** | **39** |
| Hoylake | 39 |
| Bidston | 40 |
| Wallasey Grove Road | 40 |
| Birkenhead North | 41 |
| Hamilton Square | 41 |
| Liverpool James Street | 42 |
| Birkenhead Central | 43 |
| Rock Ferry | 45 |
| | |
| **4 Birkenhead to Frodsham and Chester** | **47** |
| Woodside station | 47 |
| Mollington Street shed | 49 |
| Birkenhead Docks | 53 |
| Rock Ferry | 57 |
| Port Sunlight | 59 |
| Hooton | 60 |
| West Kirby | 65 |
| Capenhurst | 66 |
| Little Sutton | 66 |
| Helsby | 67 |
| Frodsham | 69 |
| | |
| **5 Chester and Mold Junction** | **70** |
| Approaching Chester General | 71 |
| From the east | 71 |
| From the west and south | 72 |
| Chester General station | 83 |
| 1950s | 83 |
| 1960s | 85 |
| 1970s | 92 |
| Freight and parcels | 93 |
| Departing from Chester General | 96 |
| East | 96 |
| West | 97 |
| Crossing the Canal | 103 |
| At the Roodee | 106 |
| Mold Junction engine shed | 108 |
| Chester Midland engine shed | 109 |
| Chester West engine shed | 110 |
| Chester Northgate station | 113 |
| Chester Northgate engine shed | 116 |
| | |
| **6 Chester to Denbigh and Denbigh to Rhyl** | **118** |
| Saltney Ferry | 118 |
| Broughton & Bretton | 119 |
| Mold | 120 |
| Nannerch | 121 |
| Bodfari | 121 |
| Denbigh | 122 |
| St. Asaph | 123 |
| | |
| **7 Chester to Colwyn Bay** | **124** |
| Mostyn | 124 |
| Prestatyn | 125 |
| Dyserth Branch | 127 |
| Rhyl | 129 |
| Abergele & Pensarn | 135 |
| Llandulas | 136 |
| Llysfaen | 139 |
| Colwyn Bay | 139 |
| | |
| **8 Llandudno Junction and Llandudno** | **144** |
| Llandudno Junction – the east end | 144 |
| Llandudno Junction station | 149 |
| Llandudno Junction – the west end | 153 |
| Llandudno Junction shed | 156 |
| The Llandudno Branch | 158 |
| Deganwy | 161 |
| Llandudno | 164 |
| | |
| **9 The Conway Valley line to Blaenau Ffestiniog** | **165** |
| Tal-y-Cafn & Eglwysbach | 165 |
| Llanrwst & Trefriw | 166 |
| Betws-y-Coed | 166 |
| Blaenau Ffestiniog North | 170 |
| | |
| **10 Llandudno Junction to Bangor** | **172** |
| Conway | 172 |
| Penmaenmawr | 177 |
| Llanfairfechan | 180 |
| Aber | 180 |
| Bangor | 182 |
| Bangor shed | 187 |
| | |
| **11 Bangor to Afon Wen** | **188** |
| Caernarvon | 188 |
| Brynkir | 190 |
| Chwilog | 190 |
| Afon Wen | 191 |
| | |
| **12 Bangor to Holyhead** | **195** |
| Menai Bridge | 195 |
| Britannia Tubular Bridge | 198 |
| Llanfair | 200 |
| Gaerwen | 201 |
| The Amlwch Branch | 202 |
| Holyhead | 205 |

English Electric Type '4' 1-Co-Co-1 diesel-electric No. D319 emerges from Upper Northgate Street tunnel on the approach to Chester General with an express from North Wales to London in 1963.

# North Wales, Chester and the Wirral

This map shows the ownership of the lines immediately before the 1923 Grouping.

- BIRK — Birkenhead Railway (Joint L&NWR and GWR)
- CAM — Cambrian Railways
- CLC — Cheshire Lines Committee
- GC — Great Central Railway
- GW — Great Western Railway
- L&NW — London & North Western Railway
- MER — Mersey Railway
- WIR — Wirral Railway

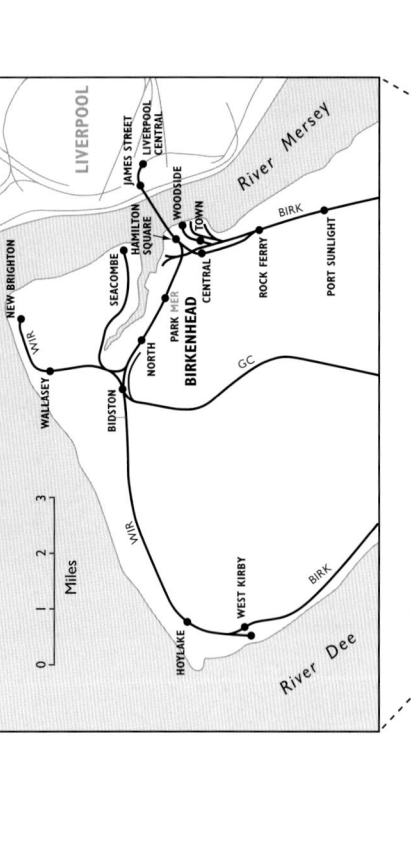

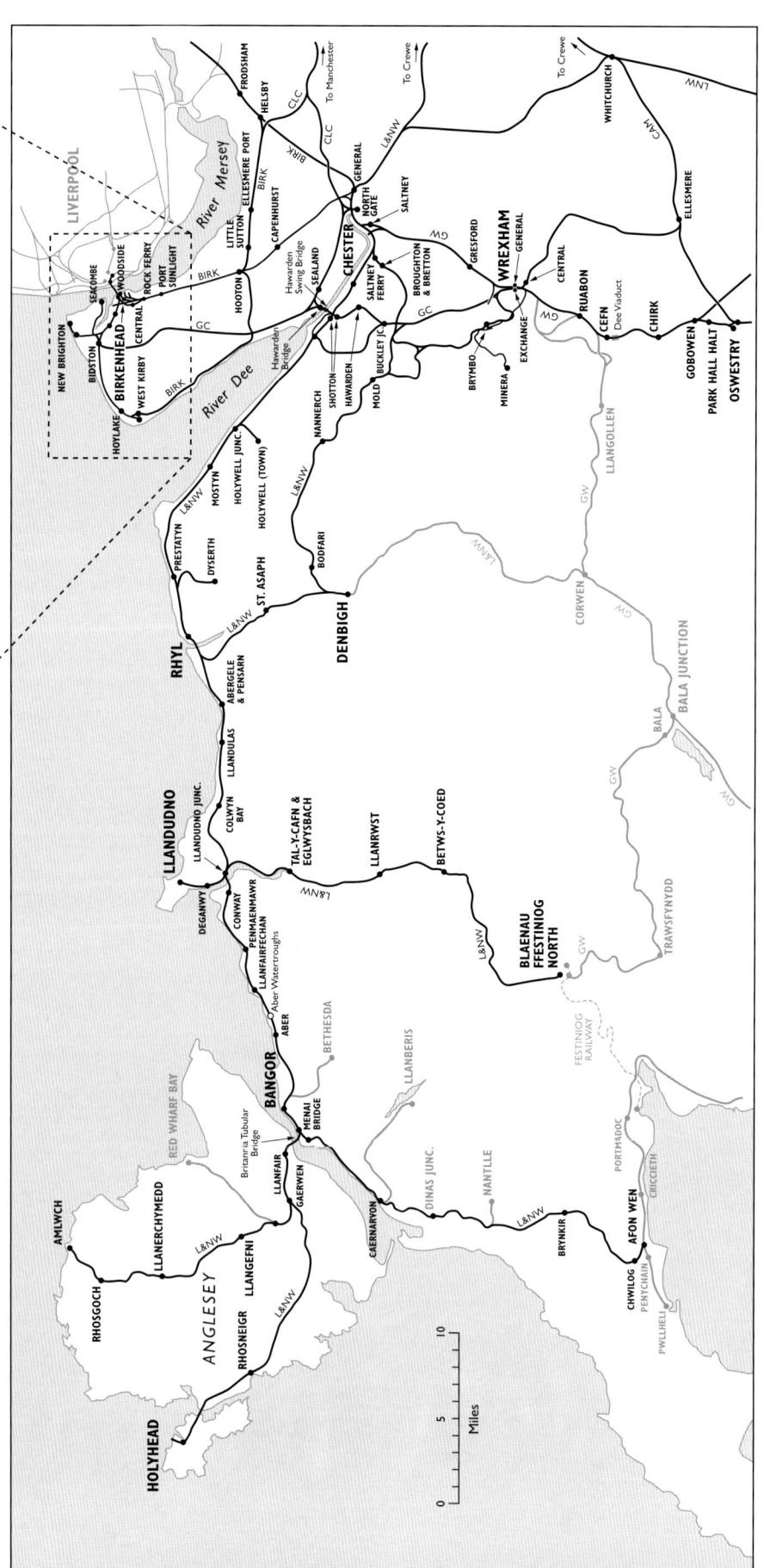

# Introduction and Acknowledgements

This is the eleventh in a series of books, depicting the first 25 years of British Railways, which will eventually cover the whole of the UK. We have been fortunate to have had access to hundreds of different pictures from which to choose the final selection presented here. At an early stage, we made the decision to include photographs spanning the early British Railways era through to the pre-TOPS diesels and electrics, although the emphasis is on that interesting transitional period of the late 1950s and early 1960s. This volume follows on from our previous book on Mid-Wales and the Cambrian Coast and covers the lines in North Wales, Chester and the Wirral peninsular. It employs the English spelling of place names which were in use by the railway during most of the period covered.

Our journey starts at Gobowen on the Great Western Railway main line from Shrewsbury going north via Wrexham as far as the outskirts of Chester before doubling back to Wrexham to pick up the former Great Central Railway line which went to the Wirral, ending on the banks of the River Mersey at Seacombe. On the way we call in at Croes Newydd and Rhosddu, the two engine sheds at Wrexham, and after crossing the Mersey at Shotton we also visit the shed at Bidston. While on Merseyside we take a close look at the Wirral electric multiple units, the pioneering main line electrified suburban system.

After a look around the docks and Mollington Street shed, we return south from Birkenhead to Chester, branching off on the way to Helsby and Frodsham. At Chester we untangle the complex of lines into General station which handled Western Region and London Midland Region services, and contrast this with the former Great Central and Cheshire Lines Committee lines which ran into their own station at Northgate. The city was served by three engine sheds with a fourth just outside the boundary at Mold Junction which handled the extensive freight traffic to and from the North Wales coast.

After the bustle of Chester, the rural line to Denbigh and up to Rhyl provides a complete contrast before we revert to the former London & North Western Railway main line and travel along the North Wales coast passing through popular seaside resorts, taking a short detour at Prestatyn down the Dyserth branch, before resuming our journey to the most important station on the main line, Llandudno Junction. There we will visit the engine shed and then travel down the two branches which start at the Junction, the short line to Llandudno itself before a longer trip down the Conway Valley line to Blaenau Ffestiniog.

Regaining the main line towards Bangor, at Conway we pass through the first of two iconic tubular bridges. Leaving Bangor we firstly go south down to Caernarvon on the branch to Afon Wen, then we cross Robert Stephenson's second tubular bridge over into Anglesey with a short trip up the branch to Amlwch before the final leg to the port of Holyhead.

Right up to the mid-1960s Summer Saturdays saw a vast amount of holiday traffic, transforming the operation of the North Wales main line as many relief and excursion trains to the coastal resorts had to be accommodated.

The motive power on the ex-Great Central lines had remained virtually unchanged for half a century until the mid-1950s when LM&SR and BR Standard engines took over from the Great Central designs. Chester General and the main lines radiating from there saw almost every class of LM&SR locomotive up to the 'Coronation' Pacifics and GWR types except only for the 'King' Class. There was a gradual replacement of the earlier designs by the later Stanier, Ivatt and BR Standard classes, a trend accelerated by the transfer of responsibility for motive power from the Western Region to the London Midland Region in 1963 which rapidly reduced the numbers of the remaining GWR engines.

North Wales was at the forefront of the introduction of diesel multiple units from 1956 onwards and these spread east to the ex-Great Central lines in 1960. Main line diesels replaced steam gradually from 1959 onwards with the English Electric Type '4' eventually becoming prevalent on the expresses along the coast to Holyhead, although steam did enjoy a brief resurgence on the former GWR route after it was transferred to the LMR. On the Wirral, the original electric units were replaced in the mid-1950s when British Railways built more of the 1930s LM&SR design already in use there, a type which was far in advance of contemporary multiple units on other Regions until the late 1960s.

### Acknowledgements

Once again, we are grateful for the expertise and enthusiasm of Steve Phillips who designed this book as well as our previous volumes in this series. We have benefitted in no small degree from the local knowledge of John Cowlishaw and Larry Davies, and from Tony Wright, a native Cestrian, for his input, particularly on the Chester chapter. Our thanks also go to Vic Smith for his help. Any errors remaining are of course entirely the responsibility of the authors and publishers.

The pictures in this volume are from the *www.Rail-Online.co.uk* collection or Rail Archive Stephenson whose pictures are hosted on the site. We have taken the opportunity to include whole page portraits which show the quality of some of these fifty- or sixty-year old photographs. This volume features many pictures taken by the late Jim Carter, the British Railways driver, one of whose favourite locations was Chester.

### References

We have consulted a number of books to provide details of locomotives and workings. In particular, the RCTS *BR Standard* and *LM&SR* series and the Irwell Press 'Book of' series have allowed us to include details of allocations and modifications. Also, the books on the lines in the area by W.G. Rear have proved useful.

*J. Allan*
*A. Murray*

# 1 – Gobowen to Chester

The North Wales Mineral Railway was formed in 1844 to build a line between Chester, Wrexham and Ruabon and in 1845 the Shrewsbury, Oswestry and Chester Junction Railway was incorporated to continue southwards from Ruabon to Shrewsbury. The two companies merged in 1846 to create the Shrewsbury and Chester Railway. The line to Ruabon was opened in December 1846 and to Shrewsbury in October 1848, with a short 2½ mile long branch to Oswestry from a junction at Gobowen following two months later. In 1854 the Shrewsbury and Chester Railway was taken over by the Great Western Railway, completing its through route from Paddington via Birmingham and Wolverhampton to Chester and thence over the joint line with the L&NWR to Birkenhead.

## Park Hall Halt

Park Hall estate was given by the owner to the military to use as their local headquarters in the First World War and in spring 1915 a military camp was constructed to train the troops. Following the owner's death the estate was conveyed to the War Office in 1920. The Hall itself was destroyed by fire in 1918 but the camp hospital continued in use, and the Baschurch Convalescent and Surgical Home, set up by Agnes Hunt, moved there in February 1921. It then became known as the 'Shropshire Orthopaedic Hospital' and later 'The Robert Jones and Agnes Hunt Orthopaedic Hospital'. It has become world renowned for its pioneering work in the treatment of all forms of physical disablement.

A BR Standard Class '2' 2-6-0 at Park Hall Halt heading north towards the junction at Gobowen in 1965. The short freight from Oswestry contains two brake vans, one a BR design and one a GWR 'Toad', sandwiching four sheeted opens branded 'Iron Ore' although most likely carrying stone from Blodwell.

With the hospital in the background, a Metro-Cammell two-car DMU, Class '101' under TOPS departs from Park Hall Halt with the shuttle service from Oswestry to Gobowen. The introduction of the DMUs to replace the steam auto-trains in 1964 increased the shuttle service to twenty-one trains daily in each direction. The Oswestry-Gobowen line was not mentioned in the 1963 Beeching Report, presumably because it was profitable, and the service continued until November 1966, nearly two years after the passenger service on the main line between Whitchurch and Welshpool had been withdrawn.

# CHAPTER 1 - GOBOWEN TO CHESTER

**Gobowen**

Gobowen was the last station in England on the Shrewsbury to Chester Railway, all the others to the north as far as the outskirts of Chester were in Wales.

GWR '54XX' Class 0-6-0PT No. 5422 propels an auto train away from Gobowen to Oswestry on 1st July 1958. The 2½ mile journey took eight minutes. Oswestry had only a single 54XX, the auto-fitted 5ft 2in. wheel variant of the standard GWR Pannier, which shared the shuttle trains with its several '14XX' 0-4-2Ts. No. 5422 was at Oswestry from November 1957, replacing No. 5401 which was withdrawn, and was itself replaced by No. 5421 from Southall when it was withdrawn in June 1960. Gobowen South Signal Box which controlled the junction is just visible on the extreme left of the picture.
*R.O. Tuck/Rail Archive Stephenson*

A southbound Class 'C' fitted freight passing through Gobowen station on 12th April 1962 headed by No. 5910 *Park Hall*. The estate after which it was named was, coincidentally, less than a mile away on the branch to Oswestry. No. 5910 was at Cardiff Canton from December 1959, moving to Oxley in December 1960 from where it was withdrawn in September 1962. Note the two BR Standard cattle wagons and the older LM&SR design built just after nationalisation on the right.

The GWR tanks on the Oswestry Branch trains were replaced by BR Standard and LM&SR 2-6-2Ts for a short time before DMUs took over in 1964. Ivatt No. 41285 had been transferred from Leamington to Oswestry in July 1963 and stayed until July 1964 when it went to Llandudno Junction. The large running-in board informs passengers arriving on the shuttle that this was the junction for 'CHESTER & THE NORTH' and 'SHREWSBURY & THE SOUTH'.

A Derby two-car DMU, later Class '108', arrives with the shuttle service from Oswestry on 21st July 1964. The coal yard at Gobowen, which was located where the photographer was standing on the Down side, was the last surviving rail-served domestic coal yard in the country.

CHAPTER 1 - GOBOWEN TO CHESTER

Passing Gobowen North Signal Box No. 6806 *Blackwell Grange* on a southbound Class 'H' freight approaches Gobowen station on 21st July 1964, as a Ford Anglia waits at the level crossing over Chirk Road with plenty of activity on the right. The 'Grange' 4-6-0s were nominally rebuilds, for accountancy and tax purposes, of withdrawn '43XX' 2-6-0s and incorporated a few salvaged parts such as wheels, motion and also the tenders. They had new frames and boilers, improved cylinders and with their 5ft 8in. driving wheels, 4in. less than the 'Hall' Class 4-6-0s, they proved useful mixed traffic engines. No. 6806 was built in September 1936 and was allocated to Worcester from 1961 until withdrawn in October 1964. Note the low signal post so the signals could be sighted below the station footbridge; the distant arm was motor worked from Weston Rhyn. To the left is the sign for the 'Hart & Trumpet' public house whose patrons had a close-up view of the passing trains and must have noticed their beer shaking as they passed!

One of the later Collett version of the Churchward '28XX' 2-8-0s with side window cab and outside steam pipes, No. 3809 approaches Gobowen station with a northbound freight as it passes Gobowen South Signal Box on 21st July 1964.

'9F' 2-10-0 No. 92152 brings a long northbound freight down the hill into Gobowen on 9th September 1965 and is approaching the crossing gates shown on page 11. It was built in October 1957 and allocated to Saltley until the end of 1966. Note the position of the centre lamps for the Class 'E' partially fitted headcode which have been moved to the right because the upper one has been lowered onto the smokebox door for safety reasons when working under overhead wires and the one on the footplate moved across so that it was aligned vertically. The first two bogie wagons are carrying brand new Mini and Morris Minor cars from the factory at Cowley near Oxford, although immediately behind the engine these are not sheeted over. Just visible in the distance is the bridge carrying the Oswestry-Whitchurch line.

## Cefn Dee Viaduct

The 1,532 ft long Cefn Viaduct across the River Dee about two miles south of Ruabon in the Vale of Llangollen had nineteen semi-circular arches of 60 ft span and reached a height of 148 ft above the river bed. A Class '108' DMU is dwarfed by the structure as it crosses with the 09.45 Chester to Wolverhampton on 15th June 1967.

## Ruabon

No. 4924 *Eydon Hall* at Llangollen Line Junction south of Ruabon with a short, four-coach northbound express was one of the first batch of the Class built in the late-1920s, entering service in May 1929. It had been transferred from Exeter to Shrewsbury in July 1962 and this picture was taken in the four months before it moved to Swindon in November 1962. The Llangollen line veered away to the right behind the first coach.

'Castle' 4-6-0 No. 5088 *Llanthony Abbey* about to depart from Ruabon with a Birkenhead-Paddington express on 29th September 1962, in the week it was withdrawn from service. This was one of the nominally 'new' engines for accountancy reasons that were actually rebuilds of withdrawn 'Star' 4-6-0s. It entered service in February 1939 replacing 'Star' No. 4068 which was withdrawn in November 1938. No. 5088 was allocated to Wolverhampton Stafford Road from 1942 until withdrawal. The extensive sidings at Ruabon are visible in the background and there is also a turntable hidden by No. 5088.

Special permission had to be given for No. 6000 *King George V* to work the annual 'Talyllyn Railway Preservation Special' from Paddington north of Shrewsbury through to Ruabon on 29th September 1962 where a packed platform is waiting expectedly. Its return to London was scheduled to take the 'King' running light from Ruabon to Shrewsbury to work a local passenger train from Shrewsbury to Wolverhampton, from where it was to run Light Engine back to Old Oak Common. Events took a different turn, however, for when No. 6000 arrived at Shrewsbury that evening, a 'Western' Class diesel-hydraulic had failed there on the 6.40pm from Shrewsbury to Paddington and No. 6000 was coupled to the diesel, assisting it and its train back to London. Ruabon had extensive sidings and a large goods shed which is on the left of the picture; Ruabon Middle Signal Box is in the background. Note the centre-balance signal used by the Great Western where sighting was difficult or space restricted next to it.

No. D1000 *Western Enterprise*, in its original and unique desert sand livery, at Ruabon with the 1.10pm Paddington to Birkenhead Woodside, which it would take through to Chester, on 23rd July 1963. By the beginning of 1964 the 2,700 diesel hydraulics had been ousted by Brush Type '4' diesel-electrics on the Paddington-West Midlands-Chester route. Brian Haresnape, who wrote extensively on design matters in the contemporary railway press, stated in the March 1962 issue of *Modern Railways* that the 'Western' design featured '*the highest standard of diesel locomotive bodyform ever produced in this country*' and was '*possibly without peer anywhere in the world today*'. The design consultant responsible for the design, Misha Black, suggested the use of stainless steel numerals and a cast crest as applied to the new a.c. electrics on the LMR, but only No. D1000 had the crests although all of the class had aluminium GWR style cast number plates which he designed. Black also wanted a (turquoise) blue livery but would not get his wish until the end of the decade when BR Rail Blue became standard. Instead a 'warm fawn/grey' which had been proposed and turned down for the Eastern Region 'Deltic' was applied to the first of the class. The second was painted in maroon, subsequently adopted for the whole class, and the next three appeared in green. The yellow warning panel was added in November 1962 and *Western Enterprise* retained its desert sand livery until October 1964 when it was repainted in maroon.
*Brian Stephenson*

As the running-in board shows, Ruabon was the junction on the Great Western's Chester-Shrewsbury main line for its branch to Llangollen, Bala, Barmouth and Pwllheli (covered in Volume 10). However, after the London Midland Region took over responsibility for the line northwards from Shrewsbury from September 1963 many of the expresses from Paddington to Chester and Birkenhead were taken over by LM&SR Stanier Class '5' 4-6-0s although the GWR 4-6-0s continued alongside them until the middle of 1964. Chester's No. 45305 heads the 5.10pm Chester-Paddington soon after the line was transferred; it was moved away to Springs Branch in November 1963. The Armstrong, Whitworth-built engine was one of eighteen of the class to survive into preservation following its purchase by A.E. Draper & Sons who owned the scrapyard at Hull which disposed of a large number of steam locomotives; apparently it was the last engine surviving from the 743 taken there to be broken up but instead was saved by the company.

The enthusiasts at Ruabon on 25th April 1964 were probably waiting for the arrival of No. 4079 *Pendennis Castle* on the Festiniog Railway AGM Special rather than this scruffy 'Grange' No. 6820 *Kingstone Grange* on a Birkenhead-Paddington service. No. 6820 was from Newport Ebbw Junction but would move to Cardiff East Dock in June 1964.

Hawksworth 'Modified Hall' No. 6994 *Baggrave Hall* with a northbound express at Ruabon on 25th April 1964. It was allocated to Shrewsbury between April 1963 and June 1964, moving to Oxley for its last few months in service. Introduced in 1944, the 'Modified Hall' had several significant changes from the original Collett engines. Larger superheaters were fitted and plate frames were used throughout, dispensing with the bolted-on extension bar frames at the front end. There were new pattern cylinders bolted directly to the mainframes, a revised smokebox saddle and plate framed bogies producing a distinctively different front-end appearance. Also, from No. 6971 onwards, the class was built with a new design of straight-sided welded tenders.

## Wrexham Croes Newydd

A lengthy northbound Class 'F' freight in the Down loop at Croes Newydd South Fork is heading towards Wrexham and probably to Saltney Sidings, Chester with Collett 'Hall' 4-6-0 No. 4946 *Moseley Hall* on 19th April 1962. It was at Shrewsbury from April 1960 until withdrawn in June 1963. The line on the right leads to Croes Newydd East Fork and yard.

Stanier '8F' 2-8-0 No. 48450 from Stourbridge Junction heads a southbound train of Shell/BP oil tankers, probably from Stanlow to the West Midlands, at Croes Newydd South Fork on 2nd October 1964 and to the right '16XX' 0-6-0PT No. 1628 waits with a short Class 'D' freight. No. 48450 was one of the class built at Swindon during the Second World War and has a GWR pattern injector. Croes Newydd shed is beyond the road overbridge in the distance.

'56XX' 0-6-2T No. 6651 pulls out of the sidings and takes the Brymbo line at Croes Newydd South Fork on 11th September 1965. It was the second of the fifty engines in the class built for the GWR by Armstrong, Whitworth in 1928. No. 6651 arrived at Croes Newydd from Pontypool Road in May 1963 and was there until withdrawn in October 1965.

CHAPTER 1 - GOBOWEN TO CHESTER

The yards and depot at Croes Newydd dealt with the traffic off the industrial and colliery branches near Wrexham. '16XX' Class 0-6-0PT No. 1660 brings a local pick-up freight along the Up loop passing Watery Road goods depot on 19th April 1962. The '16XX' panniers were the last GWR-designed engines built at Swindon, No. 1660 was built in March 1955 and went to Croes Newydd shed from where it worked for the whole of its short life, until February 1966. The signal box on the main line in the distance is Croes Newydd North Fork.

## Croes Newydd shed

Croes Newydd was the last of the Great Western Railway 'northlight' designs, a roundhouse with a central turntable for access. It was opened in 1902 in the triangle of lines at Croes Newydd. The shed was coded 84J until August 1960, then 89B, and finally 6C when the London Midland Region took over in September 1963. Its condition was allowed to deteriorate badly and it was closed in June 1967, although diesels continued to stable on the sidings of the north curve until the 1980s.

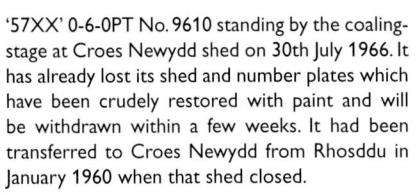

'57XX' 0-6-0PT No. 9610 standing by the coaling-stage at Croes Newydd shed on 30th July 1966. It has already lost its shed and number plates which have been crudely restored with paint and will be withdrawn within a few weeks. It had been transferred to Croes Newydd from Rhosddu in January 1960 when that shed closed.

'16XX' 0-6-0PT No. 1628 is flanked by BR Standard Class '4' 4-6-0 No. 75048 and an unidentified classmate as they slumber in the summer sun on 21st August 1966 within what was left of the roundhouse – half the roof had been removed by this time. No. 1628 was the last of the class in service and was withdrawn in September; No. 75048 lasted longer, moving to Lostock Hall when Croes Newydd closed and was in service until the end of steam in August 1968.

No. 9641 was the last GWR engine at Croes Newydd, working until 26th November 1966; it had only been there since July when it moved from Stourbridge Junction. Its last duty on that day was on the branch to Minera. The square 'roundhouse' shed had two access points from the turntable, one to the North Curve giving convenient access to the station, the other with the coaling facilities leading onto the west junction of the triangle and the Minera Branch and its sidings.

## Wrexham General

'43XX' 2-6-0 No. 6316 from Croes Newydd shed passes through the Great Western station, Wrexham General, with an Up Class 'K' freight on 11th June 1957. The coal train is probably running from Gresford Colliery to Croes Newydd Yard. The footbridge leads off picture to the ex-Great Central Railway Wrexham Exchange station (covered in Chapter 2) on the line from Seacombe, Bidston and Chester (Northgate) to Wrexham Central.

## Gresford

Stanier Class '5' 4-6-0 No. 44835 with a Paddington-Birkenhead express at Gresford on 28th September 1964. It had been at Shrewsbury since 1948 but left for the former Great Central shed at Annesley in October 1964. These expresses were the swansong of the class when in April 1966 the timings between Shrewsbury and Chester were accelerated for diesel haulage, but suitable diesels were not available and for the next year this left run-down Stanier 4-6-0s to try and maintain schedules which called for speeds in excess of 80mph. The forty-two miles from Chester to Shrewsbury included a four mile climb at 1 in 82½ up Gresford bank followed by more climbs of around 1 in 100 to 1 in 143 to near Gobowen. Speed here down the bank was restricted because of mining subsidence requiring regular lifting and packing of the track and ash ballast. The station buildings at Gresford are just visible opposite the rear of the train.

The BR Standard Class '5' 4-6-0s took their turn with the Stanier engines when the London Midland Region sheds took over the working of the expresses between Shrewsbury and Chester in late 1963 from the former GWR 4-6-0s and these had had all been displaced by mid-1964. No. 73025 heads the 15.30 Chester-Paddington at Gresford on 28th September 1964. It had been at Shrewsbury since April 1959 but left for Oxley at the start of 1965.

Also on 28th September 1964, '56XX' 0-6-2T No. 5667 runs bunker-first with a freight descending the bank at Gresford having just passed the station. It had been transferred to Croes Newydd from Barry in August 1963 and was withdrawn from there in July 1965 although the class continued to work from Croes Newydd until mid-1966. No. 5667 had been repainted in lined green when overhauled at Caerphilly in 1960 although the accumulated grime had obliterated all evidence of it by this date.

# CHAPTER 1 - GOBOWEN TO CHESTER

## Saltney

The signalman at Saltney Dee Junction Signal Box watches 'Hall' 4-6-0 No. 6924 *Grantley Hall* passing with a northbound train of only four coaches although carrying express passenger headlamps. It had been allocated to Reading since March 1959 and was paired with a Hawksworth tender from January 1961 until May 1963. The signals at Saltney were the most northerly GWR lower quadrant examples in the country. The GWR sorting sidings at Saltney were extensive and situated on both sides of the line before the junction with the L&NWR line; the exit from the Up sidings is on the left of this photograph.

Relegated to a 'K' Class unfitted freight, the pioneer Hawksworth 'County' 4-6-0 No. 1000 *County of Middlesex* moves out of Saltney Up sidings. It was the only 'County' built with a double chimney but all of the class were fitted with these between 1956 and 1959 and over the same period their boiler pressure was reduced from 280 to 250 lbs per sq. in., lowering the tractive effort from 32,580 lbs to 29,090 lbs, although they remained the most powerful GWR 2-cylinder 4-6-0s. *County of Middlesex* was transferred to St. Philip's Marsh from Bath Road shed at Bristol in September 1960 when the latter was closed for conversion to a diesel maintenance depot.

The third of the 'Modified Halls' No. 6961 *Stedham Hall* draws a long southbound Class 'D' fitted freight out of Saltney Up sidings. It was built with a Collett pattern tender but ran with the Hawksworth version from April 1963. It was allocated to Old Oak Common between April 1952 and November 1963.

The penultimate Churchward '28XX' 2-8-0 No. 2882, built in 1919, produces plenty of black smoke for the camera as it sets off with a lengthy early morning Class 'K' freight from Saltney to Shrewsbury. It was at Tyseley from September 1958 until April 1959 when it moved to Taunton.

# 2 – Wrexham to the Wirral

In May 1866 the Wrexham, Mold & Connah's Quay Junction Railway (WM&CQJR) opened a line from a point adjacent to the GWR station at Wrexham to Buckley. There it met the Buckley Railway Company line which ran from Buckley to a junction with the L&NWR Chester-Holyhead line at Connah's Quay which had opened two years earlier. The WM&CQJR took over the Buckley Railway in June 1873 and in 1887 it extended the line by 45 chains from its original terminus, which was then renamed Wrexham Exchange, to a new station, Wrexham Central. The latter was rebuilt in 1895 with five platforms, two of which were through platforms, when it also became the terminus of the Wrexham & Ellesmere Railway branch from Ellesmere, which was worked by the Cambrian Railways until the Great Western Railway took over in July 1922.

In March 1890 the WM&CQJR completed a new line, known as the Hawarden Loop, from a point about one mile south of Buckley station to Shotton via Hawarden and built a new station at Buckley Junction. At the same date the Manchester, Sheffield & Lincolnshire Railway (MS&LR) opened its line from Chester to meet the WM&CQJR at Shotton, forming a through route between Wrexham and Chester. To do this, the MS&LR line had to cross the River Dee and the Hawarden Bridge, almost 600ft long, was built at Shotton to span the river. The MS&LR had already gained access to Chester through its share of the Cheshire Lines Committee which had opened from Mouldsworth Junction to Chester Northgate in 1874.

Next, a 14¼ miles long line was opened jointly by the MS&LR and the WM&CQJR from Hawarden Bridge to the Wirral at Bidston in May 1896. The WM&CQJR had never been a financial success and most of its passenger trains were worked by MS&LR engines and coaches it failed to pay its share of the costs of the new line and the MS&LR secured the appointment of a receiver in September 1897. Following a scheme of arrangement, it was able to purchase the WM&CQJR on 1st January 1905, the MS&LR having been renamed the Great Central Railway in August 1897. Thus, the Great Central Railway, and its successor the London & North Eastern Railway, penetrated into Wales. At nationalisation, the route initially became part of the Eastern Region but was transferred to the London Midland Region at the end of 1948. Great Central Railway designs continued in use until the mid-1950s when ex-LM&SR and BR Standard engines took over.

The Seacombe Branch was built by the Wirral Railway in 1895, leaving its Bidston to New Brighton branch just north of Bidston station. In 1898, the WM&CQJR trains were extended north from Bidston to Seacombe. They were steam worked until closure in January 1960 when the service from Wrexham was switched to run to New Brighton and began operation by DMUs.

Passenger services between Wrexham and Chester Northgate were withdrawn in September 1968 and the three stations on the Hawarden Loop became unstaffed halts. Proposals in 1970 to close both Exchange and Central stations at Wrexham and to transfer the service to General station were defeated. The New Brighton service was diverted to Birkenhead North in 1976 and was cut back to Bidston in 1978; it is operated today by Transport for Wales and marketed as the 'Borderlands Line'.

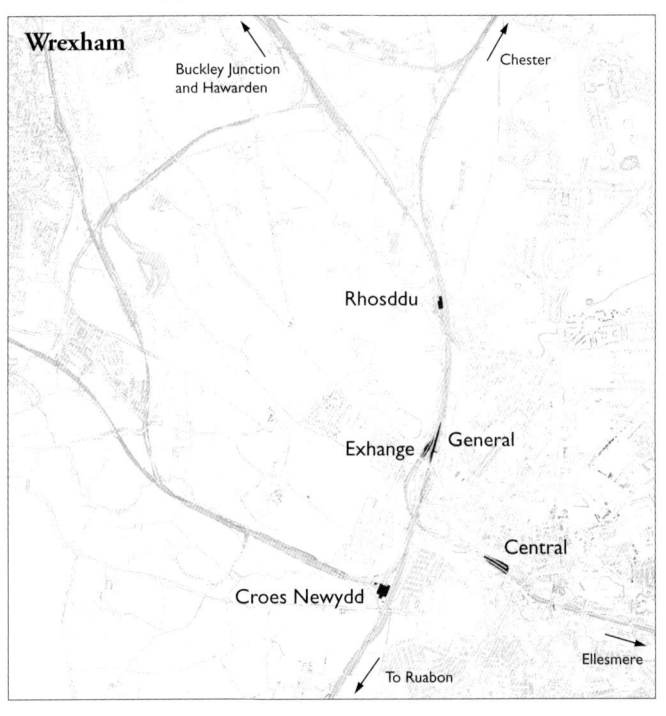

Wrexham Central station on 14th April 1952 appears almost as if nationalisation had not happened four years earlier. There are three different company names still on the timetable/poster boards, CLC, LM&S and L&NER, but no mention of the GWR which had taken over the Cambrian and therefore ran into the station with the auto train from Ellesmere. The advertisements on the left are for W. H. Samuel watches – 'If you want the right time' – and for Holiday Cruises in 1952.  *W. S. Garth/Rail Archive Stephenson*

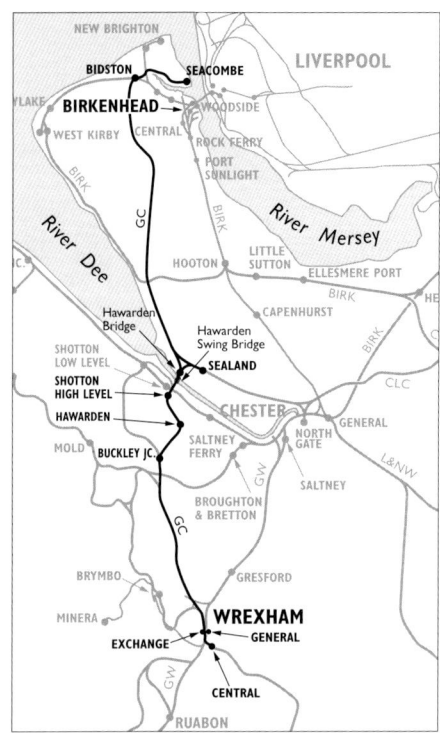

The through lines at Central station were used by the Ellesmere branch trains and in the late 1950s there were eight return trains each weekday. '14XX' 0-4-2T No. 1432 from Oswestry shed waits at Wrexham Central with the 1.30pm auto train to Ellesmere on 1st September 1962. This engine hauled the last train on the branch, the 9pm with the two auto coaches supplemented by two ordinary coaches, a week later on 8th September 1962. The DMU on the right has arrived from New Brighton.
*Robert Darlaston*

On the same day, two Derby-built DMUs, later Class '118', wait in the two terminus platforms at the north west end of the station. The one on the left is working the 1.20pm to Chester Northgate and that on the right is the 11.47am SO arrival from New Brighton. The auto trailer of the 1.30pm to Ellesmere headed by No. 1432 in one of the through platforms is just visible to the right of the building. The distinctive 135ft high tower of St. Giles' Parish Church in the background dates from 1506 and is one of the so-called 'Seven Wonders of Wales' in an 18th century poem although it is referred to as Wrexham Steeple rather than tower. Note the grounded clerestory coach in departmental use on the right.
*Robert Darlaston*

DMU Motor Composite No. M 51561 approaching Wrexham Central from Exchange in April 1967. The Derby two-car unit was allocated to Chester at this time. These units were an updated version of the Derby 'Lightweight' with a revised cab layout incorporating a headcode box; they became Class '108' under TOPS and both cars were powered to handle the steep gradients on the route. Wrexham Lager Brewery buildings are above the second coach beyond Bradley Road bridge with Wrexham Fire Station Drill Tower on the right.

## Wrexham Exchange

Ivatt Class '2' 2-6-2T No. 41235 at Wrexham Exchange with a southbound train on 30th April 1957. No. 41235 was transferred away from Rhosddu shed in June 1957, to Warrington Dallam for three months, and then to Llandudno Junction where it stayed until withdrawn in November 1962. This was the original southern terminus of the WM&CQJR with a single platform built alongside the GWR's General station. It became a through station when Wrexham Central opened in 1887 and a second platform was added. It reverted to a single platform in 1981 when it became part of Wrexham General. The poster boards on the left are still headed London & North Eastern Railway. In the background on the right a '43XX' 2-6-0 is heading north with a freight on the goods loop of the former GWR General station. In the late-1950s there were five weekday trains from Wrexham Central to Chester Northgate and ten to Seacombe.

### Rhosddu shed

The shed was built in 1912, replacing a wooden structure built by the WM&CQJR and was the only L&NER shed in Wales. It was transferred from the Eastern Region to the London Midland Region in 1949 when it had on its books ten 'N5' 0-6-2Ts, five 'C13' 4-4-2Ts, two 'J11' 0-6-0s, two 'Y3' Sentinels, one 'C14' 4-4-2T, one 'J62' 0-6-0ST and one 'J67' 0-6-0T. Rhosddu came under the Western Region in February 1958 and was closed in January 1960 when most of its allocation was transferred to the former GWR shed at Croes Newydd. It was coded 6E until 1958 when it became 84K.

Robinson 'C14' 4-4-2T No. 67442 at Rhosddu on 12th August 1951. It was built by Beyer, Peacock as GCR No. 1122 in 1907. It became No. 6122 in 1925, No. 7442 in 1946 and was allocated to Rhosddu from July 1948 until withdrawn in November 1957. It was the only one of the later Robinson 4-4-2Ts, introduced in 1907, the remainder of the Rhosddu 4-4-2T allocation being the earlier 'C13' type. Note the ancient Great Central Railway six-wheeled hand crane, built by Cravens and one of five ordered in 1907 to lift fifteen tons specifically for breakdown duties; it is coupled to a tool van of similar origin.

Rhosddu also had a single example of the Pollitt GCR 'J62' 0-6-0ST introduced in 1897. No. 68200, there on 22nd July 1951, was built at Gorton as GCR No. 883; it became L&NER No. 5883 in December 1925 and 8200 in August 1946. No. 68200 had been allocated to Rhosddu since before nationalisation and was withdrawn in November 1951.

Even though the LMR had taken over the shed in 1949, all the engines in this 1957 picture are former L&NER pre-grouping designs except for one BR Standard Class '2' 2-6-2T No. 84000. Four of the 2-6-2Ts had been transferred from Plodder Lane when passenger services between Bolton Great Moor Street and Manchester Exchange were withdrawn; they took over the passenger work from the 'C13' 4-4-2Ts. They all left for either Chester or Birkenhead by mid-1956 to work on the Wirral push-pull services (see chapter 4) and were replaced by the earlier Ivatt LM&SR version. From left to right, the other engines which can be identified are 'J67' 0-6-0T No. 68585 which was transferred from Trafford Park in April 1956, and two Parker 'N5' 0-6-2Ts No. 69362 and No. 69290 both of which had been at Rhosddu since before nationalisation. No. 68585 and No. 69362 were withdrawn in mid-1958, No. 69290 left for Tyne Dock in September 1957.

## Buckley Junction

From January 1960 diesel multiple units commenced running between Wrexham Central, Chester Northgate and New Brighton, replacing the steam services between Wrexham, Chester and Seacombe. The services were considerably improved; not only was the frequency increased but eleven minutes were cut from the journey time between Chester and Wrexham, reducing it to forty-nine minutes. Twelve powered twin-sets were allocated to Chester Midland for these services (Nos M 50924-35/51561-72), which allowed for four spare sets. The extra power was needed for the steep gradients between Shotton High Level and Buckley Junction where Motor Composite No. M51561 was photographed in the mid-1960s on a northbound service. The station was at the southern end of the Hawarden Loop with the signal box just visible in the distance.

## Hawarden

Ivatt Class '2' 2-6-2T No. 41244 pulls into Hawarden on a train from Wrexham Central in the late 1950s. It was one of eight of the class transferred to Rhosddu in the mid-1950s to replace ex-GCR 'C13' 4-4-2Ts. They took over the trains between Wrexham Central and Chester Northgate and Seacombe. Hawarden was half-way down an incline of 1 in 60 over the four miles from Buckley Junction.

## Shotton High Level

GCR 'C13' 4-4-2T No. 67436 at Shotton High Level with a train for Chester Northgate on Sunday 13th April 1952. It was built at Gorton in 1905 as GCR No. 359 and was at Northgate shed from before 1948 until withdrawn in February 1956. The station was Connah's Quay & Shotton until 1952 when it became Shotton High Level. The train appears to be running 'wrong-line' or No. 67436 may be running-round even though it was push-pull fitted.

*W.S. Garth/Rail Archive Stephenson*

Ivatt Class '2' 2-6-2T No. 41215 passes Hawarden Bridge Junction signal box as it arrives at Shotton High Level in September 1959 on a Chester Northgate - Wrexham Central service. The footpath on the left and the steps down lead to Shotton Low Level station on the L&NWR main line from Chester General to North Wales and the Hawarden swing bridge is in the background. The left-hand signal arm is for a junction with the line that ran down onto a quay on the River Dee at Connah's Quay and the two small arms are probably to enable wrong-line workings to either the quay or to Hawarden Bridge.

A few minutes later, No. 41215 waits at Shotton High Level. It was allocated to Chester Northgate from September 1953 until January 1960, except for a couple of months at Bangor in early 1954. After the shed closed in January 1960 it was transferred to Lancaster Green Ayre.

## Hawarden Bridge

GCR class 'C13' 4-4-2T No. 67435 has crossed the swing bridge and approaches Hawarden Bridge station with a Wrexham Central to Seacombe train on 1st April 1952. It was built at Gorton in 1905 and was withdrawn from Rhosddu shed in December 1952. Hawarden Bridge had three spans, two fixed of 120ft each and the northernmost swing span which was 287ft long and was hydraulically powered from the building above the engine in this picture. At the top of the tower there was a signal cabin controlling the operation of the bridge which provided a good view over the bridge, railway and river. The time taken to fully open the bridge to allow a ship to pass was 2½ minutes. There was a 4ft wide footpath on each side supported by cantilevers outside the main girders. In 1911 John Summers and Sons signed an agreement with the railway allowing employees of Summers and 'children and others bringing meals to such work people to use the footways'. Everyone else had to pay a half penny each way. This arrangement continued until 1972. River traffic declined during the mid-20th century and in the 1960s the operating mechanism was dismantled, and the swing span fixed in position; the tower was demolished by 1980.

*W.S.Garth/Rail Archive Stephenson*

Parker 'N5' 0-6-2T No. 69343 waits at Hawarden Bridge with the 2.29pm Seacombe-Wrexham on 3rd June 1956. It was at Rhosddu for a year, from November 1955 until November 1956 between spells at Trafford Park shed. *The Railway Observer* reported in 1954 that the 0-6-2Ts were preferred on passenger duties to the remaining 'C13' 4-4-2Ts when a 2-6-2T was not available. Messrs John Summers & Sons opened an iron foundry in 1896 on six acres of land to the west of Hawarden Bridge and by 1902 was producing steel using the open hearth process. Hawarden Bridge Halt was opened by the L&NER to serve the works which had expanded to 470 acres and employed over 5,000 people. The Halt was upgraded to a station in 1954. The works which had become British Steel (Shotton) in 1967 ended steel production in 1980 although it continued in use finishing coil steel produced in South Wales.

## Sealand

Ivatt Class '2' 2-6-2T No. 41215 waits at Sealand with a northbound train on the Chester Northgate-Hawarden Bridge line in the mid-1950s. It had been transferred to Northgate shed from Plodder Lane in September 1953. The station was opened in 1918 as Welsh Road Halt to serve the nearby military camp at Sealand and was opened for public use the following year. It was renamed Sealand in 1931 and was open until September 1968 when the passenger services from Chester Northgate to Wrexham and New Brighton were withdrawn.

**Bidston**

Parker GCR 'N5' 0-6-2T No. 69346 arriving at Bidston on a Seacombe-Wrexham train in the mid-1950s. It was built in 1900 as GCR No. 922 and became L&NER No. 5922 in 1925. It was renumbered again as 9346 in 1946 and received its BR number in June 1949. No. 69346 was at Rhosddu shed from December 1947 until withdrawn in September 1957. The electrified tracks curving away to the left towards New Brighton formed part of a triangular junction. The extensive Bidston goods sidings stretch out in the right distance. Note the LM&SR enamel trespass sign.

CHAPTER 2 - WREXHAM TO THE WIRRAL

In a picture taken in 1967 from the footbridge at the east end of Bidston station before the A554 road bridge was constructed, a '9F' 2-10-0 brings a train of iron ore from Bidston Docks via the triangular junction from Seacombe Junction towards the station. In September 1952 new sidings were opened at Bidston Docks with two massive transporter cranes, which are in the background of this picture, installed to unload the iron ore. A new double-line connection was put in at Bidston to improve the through running for the iron ore trains from the Docks to the massive John Summers steelworks at Shotton on the northern side of the River Dee. The 65-ton capacity bogie hopper wagons used for the traffic were owned by John Summers and a normal load over the thirteen-mile route for a '9F' was eleven wagons plus a brake van, amounting to almost 1,000 tons. Until 1963 the motive power was provided by Bidston shed but when that closed Birkenhead Mollington Street took over responsibility. Steam operation continued until November 1967 when Brush Type '4' diesel-electrics took over from the 2-10-0s.

## Bidston shed

The former Great Central Railway shed at Bidston was opened in 1896 when the line from Hawarden Bridge was completed. When the shed was transferred from the Eastern Region to the London Midland Region in January 1949 its allocation was four 'J72' 0-6-0Ts, three 'J94' 0-6-0STs and one 'N5' 0-6-2T which were used for local shunting. After completion of the modernisation work at Bidston for the iron-ore traffic in 1952, the shed's allocation increased significantly in the following years as firstly Stanier '8F' 2-8-0s and then BR '9F' 2-10-0s began to work the 1,000-ton iron-ore trains. Until 1954 these trains had been worked by Eastern Region 'O1' and 'O4' 2-8-0s from Gorton on filling-in turns. Bidston shed was coded 6F from nationalisation until its closure in February 1963.

Built at Darlington in October 1914 as North Eastern Railway No. 2184, Worsdell 'J72' 0-6-0T No. 68701 is coaled up to the brim and beyond on to the cab roof on 11th May 1952. It was allocated to Bidston from before nationalisation and was there until 1954 when it went to Normanton. The four 'J72's at Bidston had smaller chimneys fitted, 2ft 4in. high compared with the 3ft 2in. standard for the class.

LM&SR Fowler '2F' 0-6-0 dock tank No. 47164 stands in front of the coaling stage on 19th April 1953. At nationalisation it was at Birkenhead Mollington Street and was transferred to Bidston with classmates Nos 47160 and 47166 in August 1952. No. 47164 moved to Devons Road at Bow in August 1956 and ended its days as a works shunter at Horwich from November 1963 until withdrawn in September 1964.

The coaling stage is looking even more decrepit than in the picture above as 'N5' 0-6-2T No. 69339 waits there on 19th July 1955. Built at Gorton in 1900 as GCR No. 915, No. 69339 was transferred from Brunswick to Bidston in October 1950; it was withdrawn in March 1956. The later engines of the class were the first in Britain to have Belpaire fireboxes. One of the travelling cranes brought in during the mid-1950s to unload iron ore in Bidston Dock is in the left distance. The signal box on the extreme left was the ex-Wirral Railway Birkenhead North No. 2 box.

A mix of LM&SR, L&NER and BR Standards on 19th July 1955 illustrate the changes to the allocation in the mid-1950s. '9F' 2-10-0 had arrived on loan in August 1955 and was permanently transferred in June 1956 while an '8F' 2-8-0 peeps out of the shed. Tank engines were still evident with 'J94' 0-6-0ST No. 68034, which came from Birkenhead Mollington Street in September 1952 along with Nos 68013 and 68030, and two LM&SR '3F' 0-6-0Ts. No. 68034 was built by Vulcan Foundry for the War Department in 1945 and purchased by the L&NER in July 1946. The building to the right behind 'J39' 0-6-0 No. 64740 is a carriage shed.

Bidston had three '9F' 2-10-0s Nos 92045-92047, from June 1956 and they were joined in 1962 by the three engines which were built with mechanical stokers, Nos 92165-92167; all six moved to Birkenhead Mollington Street which took over the John Summers iron ore trains when Bidston shed was closed in February 1963. Nos 92045 and 92046 simmer in the shed yard in around 1961.

## Seacombe

The crew of GCR class 'C13' 4-4-2T No. 67435 enjoy a break at Seacombe before it takes the train to Wrexham Central on 14th April 1952. Built at Gorton as GCR No. 357 in 1905, it was withdrawn from Rhosddu in December 1952. The Seacombe Branch was built by the Wirral Railway in 1895, leaving its Bidston to New Brighton Branch north of Bidston station. In 1898, the WM&CQJR trains were extended north from Bidston to Seacombe. The station became Seacombe & Egremont in 1901 but reverted to plain Seacombe in January 1953. There were thirteen weekday trains in the late 1950s from Seacombe to either Chester or Wrexham. The branch passed into LM&SR ownership at the 1923 Grouping but the L&NER retained running powers for its services and strangely the LM&SR never ran trains from Seacombe. The trains were steam worked until closure of the line in January 1960, when the service from Wrexham Central was dieselised and switched to run to New Brighton. The station backed onto the Mersey and there was a ferry landing stage behind which is still there today; the twin towers of the Liver Building across the river are just visible in the centre background.

*W.S. Garth/Rail Archive Stephenson*

# 3 – The Wirral electrics

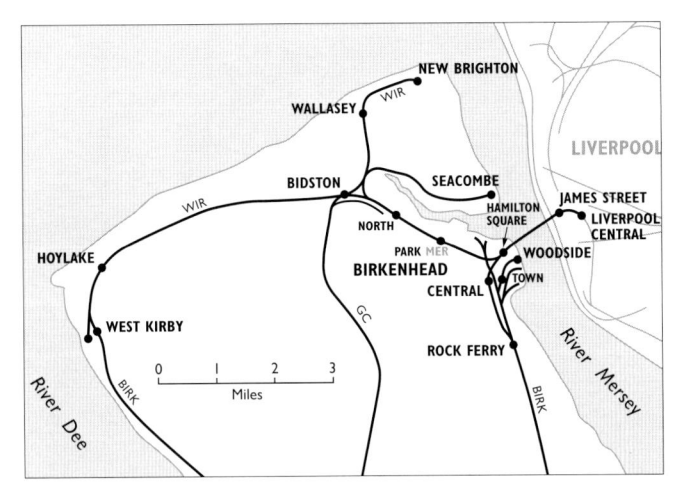

The former Mersey Railway lines on the Wirral were the first main or suburban lines in the country to be converted to electric operation, beating the London Brighton & South Coast electrification by six years. The 4.8 route miles from Liverpool Central to Birkenhead Park and Rock Ferry commenced electric working in May 1903. The Mersey Railway had opened between James Street in Liverpool and Green Lane in Birkenhead in 1886. In 1888 a branch was opened from Hamilton Square, Birkenhead to Birkenhead Park where it met the Wirral Railway and extensions from Green Lane to Rock Ferry, meeting the Birkenhead to Chester Railway, and from James Street to a low level station at Liverpool Central followed in 1891 and 1892 respectively. The line ran under the River Mersey in a tunnel with steep gradients on either approach and it was this which resulted in the conversion to electric traction to avoid the difficulties of running an extensive steam service through the foul atmosphere of the 3¾ miles of tunnels on the line which had brought the Mersey Railway to the brink of bankruptcy.

The four-rail system ran on 650 volts direct current and was supplied by the American Westinghouse Company, who were paid in shares rather than cash because they wanted to use the system as a showpiece to attract further business from other British railways. The rolling stock was designed by another US company, Baldwin, although it was built in Britain at the Westinghouse works in Trafford Park, Manchester. An intensive service of twenty trains per hour ran under the Mersey and additional stock of a similar design was added over the next thirty years as traffic expanded.

The Mersey Railway remained independent until it was nationalised in 1948, unlike the Wirral Railway which was absorbed by the LM&SR in 1923. The Wirral Railway, which in 1891 took over the two small local companies that had built lines to the west of Birkenhead, ran between Birkenhead Park and West Kirby, with a branch to New Brighton. It was never a financial success and remained steam operated, mostly with secondhand locomotives until the LM&SR brought in three '3F' 0-6-0Ts and thirteen Fowler 2-6-2Ts in the late 1920s.

In 1935 with the assistance of cheap Government loans it was decided to electrify the system using third-rail 650 volts direct current to allow through running over the Mersey Railway to Liverpool Central. The work was completed in 1938 and Metro-Cammell supplied nineteen three-car sets of modern design and appearance, contrasting with those running alongside them on Mersey Railway services.

The fourth rail on the former Mersey Railway lines was converted to third-rail operation in 1955 and the fifty year-old stock was replaced by twenty-four new sets of very similar design to the LM&SR 1938 sets. In 1985 the line from Rock Ferry to Hooton was electrified and this was further extended to Chester in October 1993.

**Hoylake**

Five years after nationalisation, a 1938-built unit was still in LM&SR crimson livery with serif numbers and lettering and roundels at Hoylake on 6th July 1953. Nearest the camera is Driving Trailer Open No. 29273. Hoylake was the original 1866 terminus of the first company, the Hoylake Railway, which ultimately became part of the Wirral Railway. The line was extended to West Kirby in 1878 where there was a connection to the Birkenhead Joint line via their Hooton Branch. Hoylake, along with three neighbouring stations, was rebuilt with reinforced concrete buildings and footbridge when the line was electrified in 1938.

## Bidston

At Bidston the electrified Wirral line met the former Great Central line from Chester and Wrexham. Two LM&SR-built units in British Railways unlined green livery, with Motor Open Brake Second No. M 28678 M nearest the camera, are on the Up and Down Goods line on Sunday 24th March 1963. The electrified running lines are on the left of the picture and the unit is running as empty coaching stock from the depot at Birkenhead North out to West Kirby. The signal box in the distance is Bidston East Junction. Note the crane runner wagon on the right, the pile of sleepers, spare rail and gas bottle which suggest there are engineering works in progress.

## Wallasey Grove Road

Motor Open Brake Second No. M 28678 M looks immaculate as it stands in Wallasey Grove Road station with a New Brighton-Liverpool Central service on 16th July 1962. Unlike No. M 28674 M on the left it has yet to receive a yellow warning panel. The nineteen three-car Wirral units designed by Stanier for the LM&SR in the late 1930s and built by Metro-Cammell were significantly ahead of their time. They employed all welded, stressed alloy construction obviating the need for heavy underframes and giving a high power-to-weight ratio; this was the first time this method had been used on other than Underground stock. In addition, each coach had four guard-operated double-leaf air-operated sliding doors and the driving coaches had modern rounded front ends; the interiors were open saloons. All the electrical equipment was slung below the floor and the motor coaches had four 135hp traction motors which were capable of starting a three-coach set on the steepest gradient on the line of 1 in 27 even if half of the motors had failed. There were buck-eye couplings but no conventional buffers and 19-core jumper cables below the central front window to permit multiple unit operation. Grove Road is one of two stations at Wallasey; the other is Wallasey Village which is on an embankment and was rebuilt after suffering damage in the Second World War.

## Birkenhead North

A New Brighton service, with Driving Trailer No. M 29273 M at the front and a very crowded cab, passes Birkenhead North No. 2 signal box on 16th July 1962. Birkenhead North station was some distance behind the unit and the lines passing to the left of the signal box served the docks.

## Hamilton Square

A Liverpool Central-bound train at Hamilton Square, the first station on the Cheshire side of the Mersey. Its underground location made photography difficult.

## Liverpool James Street

The stations below ground looked very similar to the larger London Underground stations with wide platforms and a high roof. There are few passengers waiting in this 1965 picture at Liverpool James Street looking towards Liverpool Central.

No. M 28690 M comes up the steep gradient from below the Mersey into James Street with a Liverpool Central train, probably taken on the same day in 1965 as the picture above. Note the train indicator board at the left of the picture which again is very similar to those on the London Underground. The first train is for the Rock Ferry Line as shown in the picture below and the second is for the New Brighton Line.

No. M 29279 M pulls in at just after 10.45am on a Rock Ferry service with the Liverpool Central train now in the opposite platform. The sign above the trains was advertising a local bookmaker, Bernard Murphy and Son, 'MURPHYMANSHIP ON MERSEYSIDE or the gentle art of being paid your winnings at genuine no limit'.

## Birkenhead Central

Although out of the period covered by this book, this wonderful scene is looking northwards from Birkenhead Central and would have remained the same until several years after nationalisation. Passengers are boarding Mersey Railway unit No. 29 at Birkenhead Central on a service from Rock Ferry to Liverpool Central shortly after VE Day in 1945. The second vehicle does not have a clerestory roof and was one of the ten third class steel-bodied trailers from by the Gloucester Railway Carriage & Wagon Company in 1936. The unit on the far right is a five-car set built in 1925 by Cravens of Sheffield who had also supplied two spare composite motor coaches in 1923; all had elliptical roofs and the motor coaches had domed ends.
*A.W. Croughton/Rail Archive Stephenson*

The ex-Mersey Railway stock was gradually repainted from that company's dark brown livery into BR multiple unit green, and the Coat of Arms was replaced by the BR emblem. A Mersey Railway unit arrives at Birkenhead Central from Rock Ferry on 15th May 1955. When it leaves the station, the train will immediately go into the Mersey Tunnel, 754 yards to Hamilton Square and then a further 1 mile and 1,430 yards of tunnel to Liverpool Central. The third vehicle without the clerestory roof is one of the steel bodied trailers built in 1936. The fourth rail on the former Mersey Railway lines was discontinued in 1955.

*J.F. Davies/Rail Archive Stephenson*

CHAPTER 3 - THE WIRRAL ELECTRICS

The Railway Observer commented in 1949 'Much of the Mersey stock dates back to the original electrification in 1903 and is still in amazingly good condition. It is maintained and painted at the old Mersey Railway works at Birkenhead Central'. This is borne out by unit No. 36 which was in the shed alongside the works on 2nd September 1950.
J.F.Davies/Rail Archive Stephenson

## Rock Ferry

Two views of Mersey Railway units at Rock Ferry, shortly before the last ones were taken out of service.

*Above:* All First Driving Motor Coach No. M 28412 shows the matchboard sides and the closed vestibules which replaced the original open-end gates within the first ten years following their introduction.
*J. F. Davies/Rail Archive Stephenson*

*Left:* The train has just passed the new London Midland Region Type 15 signal box which was opened in May 1957. The top of the L&NWR box it replaced is just visible to its right above the train.
*J. F. Davies/Rail Archive Stephenson*

The driver of Motor Brake Second No. M 28678 M watches the cameraman as he waits at Rock Ferry before taking out a service to Liverpool Central, a journey of only 3½ miles and mostly in tunnels, in 1960. The train is in one of the two terminal bays there and the through platforms on the left edge of the picture are for the Birkenhead-Chester line. Twenty-four three-car sets were built in 1956 to replace the life-expired former Mersey Railway stock. Metropolitan-Cammell built the motor coaches and half of the trailers and Birmingham Carriage & Wagon Co. the control trailers and the remaining trailers. They followed generally the design of the LM&SR 1938 units, but with modifications such as standard BR 4ft windows with deep sliding ventilators and also the passenger door push-buttons were repositioned alongside the doors. Both the 1938 and 1956 sets became Class '503' under TOPS and they lasted until the 1980s when Class '507' and later also Class '508' units replaced them; the last examples were withdrawn in mid-1985. The units were originally repainted from green into plain Corporate Blue in the late-1960s but this was changed in the early 1970s to the express passenger blue/grey; 'Merseyrail' branding was introduced in 1971 by the Merseyside PTE which in 1969 had taken over responsibility for transport services on Merseyside.
*Patrick Russell/Rail Archive Stephenson*

# 4 – Birkenhead to Frodsham and Chester

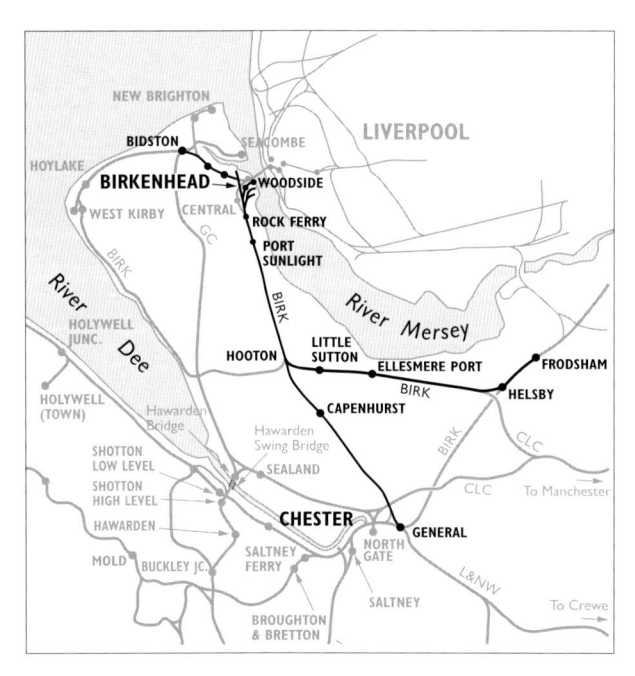

The line between Chester and Birkenhead via Hooton was opened in September 1841 by the Chester and Birkenhead Railway. It originally terminated at Grange Lane, Birkenhead but was extended in 1844 to a riverside station at Monks Ferry. The Birkenhead, Lancashire and Cheshire Junction Company was incorporated in 1846 to build a line between Chester and Walton Junction (on the West Coast mainline near Warrington) but before it was opened in December 1850 the two companies were amalgamated. In 1859 the combined company changed its name to the Birkenhead Railway and in 1861 it was vested jointly in the L&NWR and the GWR following a decade of difficult negotiations between the two companies.

A nine miles long branch from Hooton to Helsby was opened in 1863 and after the increasing traffic volume became too large to be handled at Monks Ferry a line was built from Grange Lane through a 565 yards-long tunnel to a new Birkenhead station next to the Ferry Terminal at Woodside in 1878. At the same date a large joint L&NWR and GWR engine shed was opened at Mollington Street just beyond the southern end of the tunnel. Woodside station was closed in November 1967 after through trains from Paddington had ceased earlier in the year, and services from Chester and Helsby then terminated at Rock Ferry, which was the interchange with the Wirral electric system.

**Woodside Station**

Two Mollington Street engines, Stanier '3P' 2-6-2T No. 40128 and Stanier Class '5' 2-6-0 No. 42969, at Birkenhead Woodside in the mid-1950s. London Midland engines had replaced Western Region types on the local Chester-Birkenhead trains from in early 1949. The joint station had five terminal platforms and two middle sidings and had an impressive roof with two semi-circular curved spans. In the left background is the tall obelisk-like building that houses one of the ventilation shafts for the Mersey Road Tunnel.

The Paddington-Birkenhead trains were worked north from Chester by London Midland Region engines, mostly 2-6-4Ts although Class '5' 4-6-0s and 'Crab' 2-6-0s were also used. Stanier 2-6-4T No. 42647 waits at a deserted Woodside on 4th February 1967. It had been transferred from Springs Branch to Mollington Street in July 1966 and was withdrawn in May 1967 after the through trains from Paddington ended in March.

On 12th June 1961 Derby-built diesel multiple units, later Class '108', took over the local services between Birkenhead and Helsby, Birkenhead and Chester and also Chester to Liverpool Lime Street. They provided faster timings and more trains with a regular interval pattern timetable. All the power trailer sets for these services were based at Chester West diesel depot. One of the units departs towards the tunnel, probably in early 1967. When the station closed on 4th November in that year, the only remaining services were the DMUs to Chester and Helsby.

'14xx' 0-4-2T No. 1417 has left Woodside station with empty autotrailer No. W 212, since rebuilt in preservation as Steam Railmotor No. 93, and is passing Mollington Street shed (left) with Blackpool Street signal box just visible, heading towards Rock Ferry. In 1939 there were twenty-six scheduled motor trains operating a shuttle service from either Birkenhead Woodside or Rock Ferry to Hooton or Ellesmere Port. However, by 1948 this had reduced to six motor trains working between Rock Ferry, Hooton and Helsby. The two '64XX' 0-6-0PTs which had been at Birkenhead for this work were replaced by '14XX' 0-4-2Ts, No. 1417 in July 1948 and No. 1457 in February 1949. No. 1417 was one of the few '14XX' to be painted in lined black after nationalisation. In 1949 a workmen's train was introduced linking Stanlow and Thornton with Birkenhead Woodside, but in 1951 the number of motor train services reduced to three on each weekday and dropped to two the following year. There was a change in 1954 with introduction of the 2.20pm Birkenhead Woodside to West Kirby which then formed the 3.38pm to Rock Ferry. The 1956 summer timetable saw a significant expansion of motor train services on the Wirral, particularly of evening services between Hooton and Helsby, but the two 0-4-2Ts would play no part in operating these services, both engines going into store in June, initially at Birkenhead and from March 1957 at Bidston. They were replaced by two LM&SR Ivatt 2-6-2Ts which were themselves replaced within a few weeks by two BR Standard 2-6-2Ts.

## Birkenhead Mollington Street shed

The depot at Mollington Street which opened in 1878 was shared between the London & North Western Railway and the Great Western Railway, each having eight roads of the sixteen-road through shed, divided by a common party wall. The shed originally had a northlight roof but the L&NWR side was changed to longitudinal pitches in 1938. The extensive yards serving the Birkenhead Docks required a large number of shunting engines in addition to larger tank engines for the local services and tender locomotives for freight work.

At nationalisation in 1948, Mollington Street came under of the responsibility of the London Midland Region, and from 1953 there was a slow decline in the Great Western motive power although former GWR engines continued to be allocated there until the early 1960s. In 1950 it had an allocation of ninety-four locomotives: forty GWR designs comprising six 'Grange' 4-6-0s, five '43XX' 2-6-0s, nine '41XX' 2-6-2Ts, seventeen 0-6-0PTs, two '14XX' 0-4-2Ts and a '47XX' 2-8-0. LM&SR classes totalled fifty made up of ten '8F' 2-8-0s, seven Stanier 2-6-0s, four ex-L&YR 0-6-0s, nine Stanier 2-6-2Ts and twenty 0-6-0Ts (including Fowler '2F' 'Dock Tanks') and there were four 'Austerity' ex-WD 2-8-0s.

Mechanical coaling and ash-handling plants were installed in 1954 to replace the manual methods in use until then; a double storage water tank holding 100,000 gallons with four additional water cranes was added and electric lighting replaced the original gas lights. There was little change in the allocation until the arrival of diesel shunters in 1956 to replace the '2021' panniers and the LM&SR Dock Tanks, except for the replacement of the MR '1F' 0-6-0Ts by new 0-4-0STs in 1954. The arrival of LM&SR 2-6-4Ts displaced by DMUs in the Manchester and Birmingham areas resulted in most of the remaining ex-GWR engines except for the 'Grange' 4-6-0s being stored by the end of that year. By April 1965 only five classes were represented, five LM&SR 2-6-4Ts, eleven 'Crab' 2-6-0s which had replaced the Stanier 2-6-0s, nine '3F' 0-6-0Ts, eighteen '8F' 2-8-0s and thirty-two '9F' 2-10-0s, a foretaste of what was to come later in the year when the '9F' stud increased to fifty-five. Mollington Street had the code 6C from 1948 until September 1963 when it became 8H. The shed closed to steam on 5th November 1967 after the closure of Birkenhead Woodside station following the withdrawal of through services to London Paddington in March, and the conversion of the Bidston Dock to Shotton Iron Ore trains to diesel operation.

GWR '28XX' 2-8-0 No. 2832 from Oxley in the GWR half of the shed at Birkenhead in 1951. 'Grange' No. 6841 *Marlas Grange* in the background was transferred to Mollington Street from Banbury in July 1950.

*Kenneth Field/
Rail Archive Stephenson*

Built by Kerr, Stuart, the Stoke-on-Trent locomotive builder, in May 1930, '57XX' 0-6-0PT No. 7714 was at Birkenhead from December 1937 until December 1958 when it moved to Rhosddu shed at Wrexham. The snap-head rivets on the side tanks show that this was not a product of Swindon, which produced its new panniers with flush rivets and welded joints. After withdrawal in January 1959, No. 7714 was sold to the National Coal Board for use at its Penallta Colliery near Rhymney in South Wales. Although initially used daily, the long wheelbase proved unsuitable for the tight curves in the track there and so it mostly acted as a spare engine. It was purchased by the Severn Valley Railway Association in 1973 and is now owned by the 'SVR Pannier Tank Fund'; No. 7714 is operational on the Severn Valley today.

'0F' 0-4-0ST No. 47006 in front of the ex-L&NWR half of the shed with its multiple pitched roof on 30th March 1956 sandwiched between GWR '2021' 0-6-0PT No. 2107 and another of the same class. It was one of five built at Horwich Works in late 1953/early 1954 to replace the ex-Midland Railway '1F' 0-6-0Ts which usually worked around Morpeth Dock and was allocated from new to Mollington Street. They were a development of the 0-4-0 saddle tanks, Nos. 7000-7004, built by Kitson & Co. of Leeds for the LM&SR in 1932 to what was essentially one of the company's standard designs, albeit with certain LM&SR fittings. As with the larger 0-6-0 dock tanks, they had outside cylinders. Kitsons went out of business shortly before the Second World War and the British Railways-built engines were essentially to the same design, but with smaller saddle tanks and larger side bunkers than the 1932 engines. Note the former Great Western half of the shed behind the pannier tank on the right still has its northlight roof.

CHAPTER 4 - BIRKENHEAD TO FRODSHAM AND CHESTER

'2021' 0-6-0PT No. 2069 at the entrance to the shed on 19th September 1958 with the Blackpool Street carriage sidings and Grange Lane Goods Sidings curving away to the right. It arrived in February 1955 from Carmarthen and worked for almost four years before withdrawal in April 1959, going into store from November 1958, and was the last of the class to remain in service. No. 2069 went briefly to Wolverton Carriage & Wagon Works as temporary works shunter in mid-1957. It has no warning bell for working in the docks and at this date was shed pilot after the arrival in 1956 of the Hudswell, Clarke diesels, which took over the dock shunting duties from the pannier tanks. Note the large rust hole in the upper corner left side of the bunker.

Now-preserved 'Modified Hall' No. 6990 *Witherslack Hall* inside the shed on 20th August 1961. It had been allocated to Old Oak Common since the end of 1951 and was built with a Hawksworth flat-sided tender but ran with the Collett type from 1952 onwards. Until the end of 1962 Old Oak Common engines worked the Paddington-Birkenhead freights after which they were taken over by Shrewsbury shed. No. 6990 represented the Western Region in the mixed traffic category during the 1948 Locomotive Interchange trials but was restricted to its home line and to the L&NER Marylebone-Manchester route because its width over cylinders was too great for the other test routes. *Witherslack Hall* was rescued from Woodham's scrap yard at Barry Docks in 1975 and was restored at the Great Central Railway where it has been based ever since.

A line-up of former LM&SR engines without a '9F' in sight in 1967, although a Brush Type '4' just creeps into the picture. From left to right are Class '5' 4-6-0 No. 44780 which had arrived from Shrewsbury in March, then two '8F' 2-8-0s, No. 48205 was built for the LM&SR by the North British Locomotive Company in July 1942 and 48365 was built by the LM&SR at Horwich Works in September 1944. Both engines were transferred from Heaton Mersey, arriving in January 1966 and October 1965, respectively. All three have long since lost their cast shed plates and have lowered upper lamp irons with repositioned centre irons below. One of the duties of the '8F' 2-8-0s was trip working of oil tank trains between Hooton and Stanlow oil refinery, the main line engines being attached/detached at Hooton and running Light Engine from/to Birkenhead. On the left, a Brush Type '4' and a Drewry 0-6-0 diesel-mechanical shunter are in the diesel part of the shed which was built on four of the former L&NWR roads.

'9F' 2-10-0 No. 92167 on shed in 1967 with No. 92123. The first '9F' 2-10-0s to be allocated to Birkenhead were the six transferred from Bidston in 1963 when that shed closed and the John Summers' workings were taken over by Mollington Street. One of these was No. 92167 which arrived with the other two former mechanical stoker-fitted engines, Nos 92165 and 92166; all three had been allocated to Saltley for the overnight fitted freight workings over the Settle & Carlisle line to Carlisle. By August 1965 no less than fifty-five of the class were allocated to the shed, many of which came from the LMR Midland Division, including all of the former Crosti-boilered engines; No. 92123 had come from Leicester in April 1965.

*Left:* Devoid of its front numberplate No. 92070 has just topped up its tender from the 1950s-built coaling tower. It was originally a Midland Division engine before moving to Warrington Dallam in March 1965 and then two months later to Birkenhead.

Originally No. 11148 and renumbered to D2509 in March 1961, the nearest to the camera of five 204 bhp 0-6-0 Diesel Mechanical shunters built by Hudswell, Clarke & Co. Ltd at Leeds. It had been at Birkenhead since June 1956 along with nine others of the class. They first started work at the docks on 26th April 1956, when No. 11120 was tested for clearances, and they quickly replaced the LM&SR Dock Tanks which went into store at Bidston and they took over most of the GWR '2021' class duties. All were transferred away at the end of 1966/early 1967 and were withdrawn by August 1967. Interestingly the diesels are in the steam part of the shed rather than the diesel area on the left.

## Birkenhead Docks

By 1955 all of the surviving members of the GWR '2021' Class 0-6-0PTs were concentrated at Birkenhead where there were still no suitable replacements for their duties in the Docks. No. 2107, in the Docks on 12th August 1953, was transferred from Croes Newydd in May 1953 and was at Mollington Street until withdrawn in June 1956. It was one of the final sixty of the class which were built with open cabs, saddle tanks, domeless boilers and Belpaire fireboxes; it was rebuilt with a domed boiler, pannier tanks and an enclosed cab in March 1936.

Two railwaymen and a Mersey Docks & Harbour Board policeman who controlled the crossing enjoy a chat with one of the crew of No. 47166 as it stands in front of the Royal Duke Hotel at Duke Street crossing on 2nd January 1956. No. 47166 was one of ten outside-cylindered short wheelbase 0-6-0Ts built by the LM&SR in 1928/9 for use in dockyards and depots where the track curvature was severe, but a powerful shunting engine was needed. The rear coupled axleboxes were carried in Cartazzi slides and the coupling rods had ball joints; this allowed the engines to negotiate a two chains radius curve. They were originally numbered 11270-11276 but were renumbered as 7100-7109 in 1934 and again in 1939 to 7160-7169. The hostelry dated back to at least 1866, changing its name from the Duke's Head Hotel to The Royal Duke Hotel by 1877; it was a Birkenhead Brewery pub selling Whitbread beers until it closed in the 1970s.

Mollington Street was the final bastion for the 'GWR '2021' Class 0-6-0PTs with at least ten there during the early 1950s and No. 2099 had moved there from Hereford in February 1952. At Cavendish Sidings in May 1954 a few days before withdrawal, it still has a large bell in front of the dome for working in the docks at Birkenhead, although the operating cable has been removed. No. 2099 was built with a round top firebox and saddle tanks in September 1901 and was rebuilt with riveted pannier tanks and an enclosed cab in 1928. One hundred and forty of the class were built between 1897 and 1905 at Wolverhampton Works as saddle tanks. They were a development of the '850' Class 0-6-0 saddle tanks with a longer wheelbase but were still able to traverse curves down to 3½ chains radius, hence their use in the docks at Birkenhead. The British Railways-built '16XX' panniers were built as replacements for this class, with identical wheelbase and wheel diameter but strangely none found favour at Birkenhead Docks.
*E.V. Fry/Rail Archive Stephenson*

0-6-0 Diesel Mechanical shunter, later Class '04' under TOPS, No. D2235 is shunting at Morpeth Dock in June 1968. It was built by the Vulcan Foundry at Newton-le-Willows in 1956 using parts supplied by the Drewry Car Company in London and was based on the Eastern Region until 1964. Originally numbered 11154, it was renumbered as No. D2235 in August 1959 and was transferred to Birkenhead from the Western Region in October 1966, but was only there for less than two years and was withdrawn in April 1968. The Southern-designed plywood van is looking very tatty with a partially un-felted roof, and there is packing straw all over the yard; we tend to forget how much straw was used in packing up to the late 1960s.

Swindon-built Class '03' 204bhp diesel mechanical shunter No. D2372 is coming off the main line from Birkenhead into the docks at Canning Street with a trip working in June 1968. In the background is the Neptune Works, Bridge Street factory of A. Rutherford and Co. founded in 1853. They were 'Shipbuilders and Repairers, Engineers, Boilermakers, Steam Yacht and Boat Builders, Ship and Yacht Outfitters. Specialities: Light Draft Steam and Motor Vessels of all kinds, all descriptions of small craft, ship repairs of all kinds', most of which is written on the sign in the background. Note the dot after the 'D' before the stock number of D2372, a feature of the Swindon-built diesel shunters. It was at Birkenhead from April 1964 until April 1970 when it went into store at Springs Branch prior to withdrawal in November of that year. The photographer was standing immediately in front of Canning Street North signal box and the queue of cars is waiting for the train to clear the level crossing.

Probably on the same day as in the picture overleaf, two railwaymen climb aboard No. D2375 as they appear to be running along the cobbled Tower Road. The locomotive is moving towards the hydraulically operated bascule bridge over the connection between the East Float (on the left) and Egerton Dock (to the right). Canning Street level crossing on the previous page is behind the photographer. The bridge was one of four for both road and rail traffic from Birkenhead across to Wallasey, leading to the route being christened as the 'Four Bridges Route'. Only one survives today as an operational bridge to maintain access to The Float for shipping. The modern building to the right was a Police Station with the twin clock towers of the Liver Building across the Mersey visible further to the right of the picture. No. D2375 was at Mollington Street for almost seven years, from September 1961 until withdrawn in May 1968. The piece of card wedged for some reason behind the bonnet handles says 'Radio Times'.

# Rock Ferry

Stanier 2-6-4T No. 42564 at Rock Ferry with the 2.40pm from Birkenhead to Paddington formed of ex-GWR coaches on 10th April 1954. It was at Edge Hill from October 1947 until 1960, except for a month on loan to Springs Branch in 1948 and for a month to Holyhead in late 1956.

A decade on and the 2-6-4T has changed from a Stanier to a British Railways-built Fairburn one, the coaches are all BR Mark 1s. The station gas lamps have been replaced with electric, the track is now re-laid with flatbottom rail and the signal re-painted. All subtle changes but the provision of a new high-rise block is fundamentally different, heralding the new age of high-density living. Fairburn 2-6-4T No. 42202 with an express from Birkenhead to Paddington was originally a Scottish Region engine until it was transferred to Chester in February 1960. Eight months later it went into store, was reinstated after six months and loaned to Stoke for a month; it was withdrawn in May 1965.
*Patrick Russell/Rail Archive Stephenson*

A northbound train headed by BR Standard Class '4' 2-6-0 No. 76020 in November 1965. The mogul moved to Chester in July 1965 from Stoke and was withdrawn in April 1966. Note the Wirral electric unit in the platform on the right, providing passengers with a convenient interchange to reach the wider Merseyside area. The station was as convenient for passengers as Birkenhead Woodside and hence in 1967 the services from Chester and Helsby were cut back to terminate there.

A former Crosti-boilered 2-10-0 No. 92024 approaches Rock Ferry with a sizeable Class '7' freight from the docks in November 1965. By mid-1965 five of the former Crosti engines had been transferred to Birkenhead, including No. 92024; all ten of them were there at some time in the mid-1960s.

Stanier Class '5' 4-6-0 No. 45310 from Shrewsbury is ready to depart from Rock Ferry with a northbound train on 4th February 1967. The teenage spotter leaning out of the first coach is clutching not just his notebook but also a copy of Ian Allan *Pre-Grouping Gazetteer*. He must be studying the route very closely!

## Port Sunlight

A Stanier 2-6-4T with a Paddington-Birkenhead express approaches Port Sunlight station on 27th December 1966. Off camera to the left is the Lever Brothers' soap works which had an extensive internal railway system and a model village for the employees. The station was opened as Port Sunlight Halt for use by the workers in 1914 and it became a public station in May 1927.

Two Metro-Cammell two-car DMUs arriving at Port Sunlight with a northbound service to Rock Ferry in the early 1970s. In the background is the Unilever Research & Development building. The Unilever group was created in 1929 by a merger between Lever Brothers and the Dutch 'Margarine Unie' (Margarine Union). After the Second World War Unilever expanded considerably with innovations such as frozen fish fingers and the development of its food and non-food products. In the 1950s the Research Division at Port Sunlight took over responsibility for both UK and Dutch laboratories, and hence played an important role in this work. The bridge in the distance was an internal walkway, now demolished, between the two parts of the factory. The platform from which this picture was taken was a new one built on the site of the Down Fast line when the Fast lines were removed; Port Sunlight was unusual in previously only having platforms on the Down Slow and Up Fast lines, the two outer tracks.

## Hooton

The summer timetable commencing on 11th June 1956 saw a significant expansion of motor train services on the Wirral, particularly of evening services over the nine miles between Hooton and Helsby. Birkenhead's GWR '14XX' 0-4-2Ts had been put into store and their duties were taken over by two Ivatt 2-6-2Ts transferred from Bangor, but these were themselves replaced a month later by two BR Standard 2-6-2Ts, Nos 84000 and 84004. The former is on one of the Helsby services, probably in 1960 before they taken over by diesel multiple units in January 1961.

Hughes/Fowler '5P4F' 2-6-0 No. 42782 on a pick-up goods at Hooton on 16th September 1965. It was built in 1927 as LM&SR No. 13082 and renumbered as 2782 in April 1935. No. 42782 was allocated to Birkenhead from September 1963 until withdrawn in December 1966. The 'Crab' 2-6-0s had been allocated to Mollington Street since late 1931 and were there up to the beginning of 1967, mostly on freight work by that time, although with occasional passenger work right up until the end of 1966; Nos.42727 and 42942 were the last two to leave.

CHAPTER 4 - BIRKENHEAD TO FRODSHAM AND CHESTER

The Paddington expresses between Birkenhead and Chester were worked for over a decade mainly by LM&SR 2-6-4Ts such as No. 42613 leaving Hooton with an Up train on 29th April 1966, only a month after it was transferred to Birkenhead having been in store at Carnforth since August 1965. It was built by the North British Locomotive Company for the LM&SR in January 1937, one of seventy-three purchased using Government-guaranteed loans, and was withdrawn in April 1967.

With a crudely chalked headcode on the smokebox and devoid of its *Britannia* nameplates, No. 70000 leaves Hooton with a parcels train on the line towards Helsby on 29th April 1966. It was transferred to the LMR from the Eastern Region in March 1963, and had reached its final shed, Newton Heath, in March 1966. It has a lowered top lamp holder and smoke deflectors with hand holds in place of the original handrails. *Britannia* was selected for preservation in the National Collection because of its importance as the first BR Standard engine in service but was badly damaged while in store at Preston Park, Brighton. It was replaced by 70013 *Oliver Cromwell* and was put up for sale. *Britannia* was purchased in 1971 by The Steam Locomotive Preservation Company Ltd and has subsequently had several owners. It is now owned by Jeremy Hoskin's 'Royal Scot Locomotive and General Trust' and has worked on the main line in the past decade.

One of four of the BR Standard Class '4' 2-6-0s at Chester by summer 1966, No. 76047 on a Chester bound Class '7' freight on 29th April 1966. It had been transferred from Bescot in March 1966 and was withdrawn from Chester at the end of the year. The four-track section ended at Ledsham Junction, half a mile south of Ledsham station, which had been closed in 1959.

Having run round its train at Hooton, '9F' 2-10-0 No. 92089 runs tender-first on the Down line from Hooton with empty Gulf oil tanks for the oil refinery at Stanlow (Ellesmere Port) and is about to pass under the Heath Lane road bridge on 29th April 1966. No. 92089 was originally an Eastern Region engine, arriving at Birkenhead in January 1965.

An interesting block train of bogie flats partially loaded with almost out-of-gauge, two-tier loads is heading towards Chester hauled by No. 92103 on 29th April 1966. The vehicles appear to have been adapted from ex-GWR 'Bocars' for the cargo so it must have been a regular traffic flow which we suspect was associated with car parts from the nearby Vauxhall Ellesmere Port site. The '9F' was one of a number of the class transferred to Birkenhead from Leicester Midland in April 1965. Another of the class waits at the signals on the right with a train off the Helsby line.

One of the final batch of English Electric Type '4' diesel-electrics, No. D380 has come off the Ellesmere Port line, which curves away to the left, onto the Fast line as it approaches the south end of Hooton station with a block oil train on 22nd April 1967. It will run round the train, which has a brake van at each end, before heading in the opposite direction past Hooton South Junction signal box towards Chester. Note the short arms on the bracket signal.

In a picture taken at ground level by the Heath Lane road bridge south of the station on the line to Helsby, a filthy Stanier Class '5' No. 45412 brings a train of new Vauxhall 'Viva' cars from the nearby factory on 15th June 1967. These were assembled from 1964 until 1979 at a plant opened by Vauxhall in 1963 on a 400 acre site at Hooton Park and today it builds the 'Astra' model there for its current owner, Peugeot-Citroen. No. 45412 had been transferred to Speke Junction, hence the 8C crudely daubed on the smokebox door, but was nearing the end of its days and was withdrawn in August 1967.

On the same day, a Metro-Cammell DMU goes towards Little Sutton while snowplough-fitted Stanier '8F' 2-8-0 No. 48218 approaches Hooton with a freight running under Class '7' Mineral or Empty Wagon lamps. No. 48218 was built in September 1942 by the North British Locomotive Company and had been allocated to Rose Grove since June 1965; it was withdrawn from there in September 1967.

## West Kirby

'51XX' 2-6-2T No. 5176 waits to depart from West Kirby with the 2.45pm to Hooton on 31st May 1952. The train appears to have been brought in by another 'Prairie' at the far end of the four-coach set. The twelve miles long LM&SR/GWR Joint single-track branch from the main line at Hooton was opened in 1886 and ran across the Wirral before turning north and up along the Dee estuary. There was a physical connection with the electrified Wirral Railway line from Birkenhead which terminated in platforms beyond the goods yard on the left, where a Fowler '3F' 0-6-0T is shunting. There was siding accommodation for stabling six three-car electric sets as well as space for four more in the platforms. The joint station was controlled by the Wirral line's signal box which is directly behind the train in this picture. In 1950 there were ten weekday trains in each direction, down from twelve a year before nationalisation; traffic continued to decline over the next few years and three of the intermediate stations were closed in 1954. The Hooton-West Kirby Branch was closed to passenger traffic in September although a freight service lingered on until May 1962 and the track was lifted in 1964. The trackbed became a twelve-mile long footpath/bridleway known as the Wirral Way in the newly created Wirral Country Park, the first designated country park in the UK, which opened in 1973.

## Capenhurst

Running bunker-first, Fairburn 2-6-4T No. 42224 heads the 11.40am Birkenhead to Paddington express south of Capenhurst on the outskirts of Chester in summer 1965. It began life in 1946 on the London, Tilbury & Southend, moving to the London Midland Region after displacement by electrification in June 1962, initially at Stoke and then at Chester between July 1965 and September 1965 before moving to Fleetwood.

## Little Sutton

Taken from the station footbridge '9F' 2-10-0 No. 92135 from Croes Newydd approaches Little Sutton station with an eastbound Class '8' freight. It was at the Wrexham shed for just five months, between May and October 1966; No. 92135 had been at Saltley from new in June 1957. The signal with dual arms on the post is converted L&NWR and the trespass sign is a L&NWR and GWR joint notice.

## Helsby

A short Class 'J' (mineral or empty wagon) northbound freight from Chester passes through Helsby headed by BR Standard Class '2' 2-6-0 No. 78032. The picture was taken while it was at Chester, between May 1960 and September 1963, after which it moved to Bangor. The four members of the class there worked mainly on local passenger services along the North Wales coast. The line to the right goes to Ellesmere Port, Hooton and Birkenhead.

Derby two-car DMU, later Class '108', Nos M50627 and M56213 at Helsby on a Birkenhead service on 25th April 1964. This set had been based at Chester since 1961 when the DMUs took over the local services from steam. Note the co-acting signal on the main line visible above and below the footbridge.

Stanier Class '5' 4-6-0 No. 44917 heads a Class '6' freight through Helsby towards Chester on 22nd April 1967. It has a painted 6A shed code and had been at Chester since April 1966 having spent the previous seven years at Mold Junction.

Diesel Multiple Units occupy three of the four platforms at Helsby in the mid-1960s. On the left is a Derby twin-power car unit which has arrived in Platform 4 from Birkenhead and a Metro-Cammell set is in Platform 3; just visible on the right and signalled to depart towards Frodsham is another Derby unit in Platform 2 on the line from Chester. Both the units on the left have tail lamps and the driver of one of them is attending to something, so it is possible that the two units are going to be coupled up.

# CHAPTER 4 - BIRKENHEAD TO FRODSHAM AND CHESTER

## Frodsham

'Royal Scot' 4-6-0 No. 46148 *The Manchester Regiment* departs from Frodsham with a Manchester-Llandudno express on 25th April 1964. When built in 1927 it was named *Velocipede* which name it kept until June 1935. No. 46148 had only six months left in traffic before it was withdrawn from Holyhead in November 1964.

Stanier '8F' 2-8-0 No. 48457 on the 1.35am Healey Mills to Birkenhead Class '6' freight approaches Frodsham Junction having passed through Halton station on the line from Warrington, probably in 1965. It was one of the Swindon-built engines, entering service in October 1944, and was at Speke Junction from March 1965 until withdrawn in September 1966.

# 5 – Chester and Mold Junction

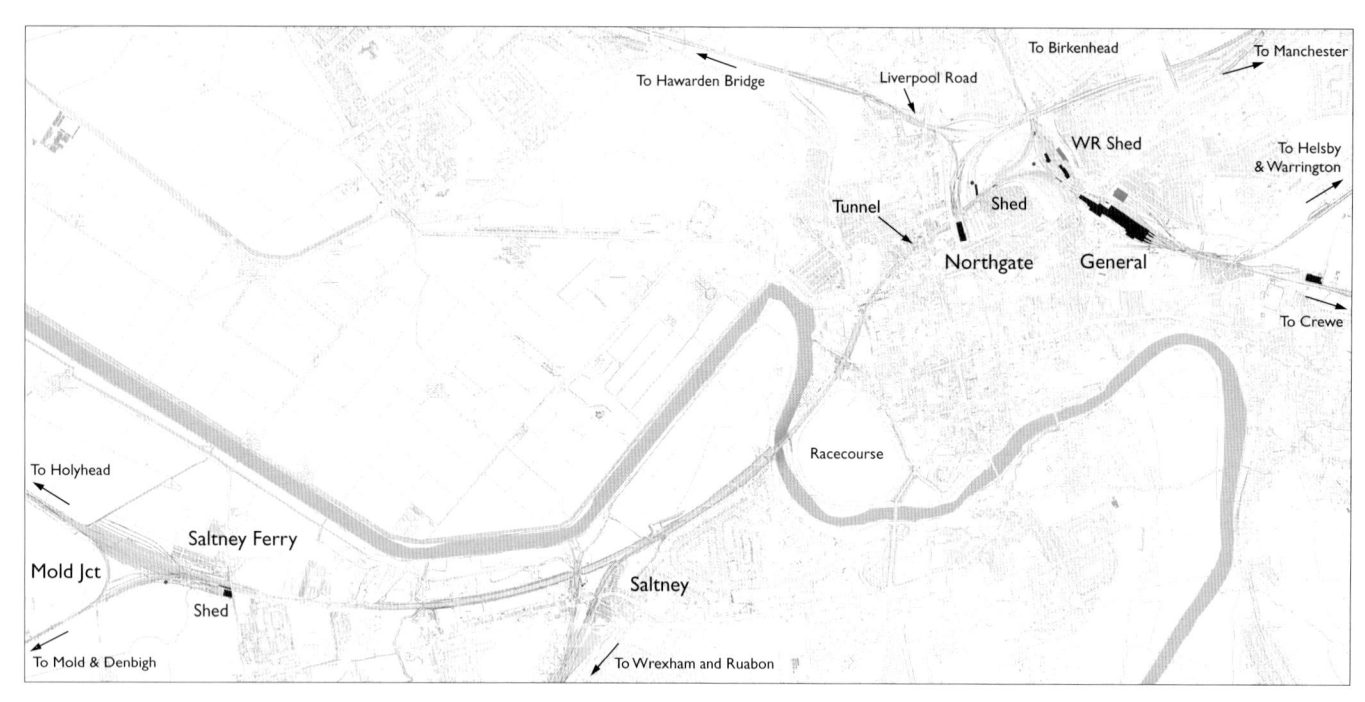

The Chester & Birkenhead Railway, opened in 1841 and later renamed the Birkenhead Joint Railway, met the Chester & Crewe Railway, which had opened the year before, near the site of the present Chester General, a joint station which was opened in 1848 and was renamed as such in 1875 to distinguish it from the new Cheshire Lines Committee station at Northgate. Also in 1848, the Shrewsbury & Chester Railway reached Saltney to the west of Chester and had running powers over the 1 mile 23 chains into Chester of the Chester & Holyhead where it met the Joint line outside General station. The station became the joint property of the L&NWR and the GWR and the 'General' suffix was dropped in 1969 after Northgate station was closed.

In 1875 the Cheshire Lines Committee, which was jointly owned by the Great Northern, Great Central and the Midland Railways, completed its route into Chester from Mouldsworth Junction on its line from Northwich to Helsby. Its station at Northgate was more convenient for the City Centre than the joint General station.

There was a third station, Liverpool Road, immediately outside Northgate on the Great Central line to Hawarden Bridge after the triangular junction, but this was not well utilised since it was very near to Northgate and closed in December 1951.

The Holyhead line leaves the north end of General station and immediately curves to the west passing through two short tunnels and then runs beside the Roodee where the Chester races are held before crossing the River Dee on an iron bridge with three 100ft spans. Then at Saltney, the GWR line to Wrexham, Ruabon and Shrewsbury curves away to the south. On the four track section between Saltney Junction and General station Western Region trains from London Paddington ran in the same direction as London Midland Region trains to London Euston and vice versa.

The western end of Chester General which handled both the departing Up and arriving Down Western Region trains as well as the London Midland Region services in both directions was always busier than the LMR-only eastern end, although it was rare to see three trains together in a line as in this picture taken in the second half of 1962.

Stanier Class '5' 4-6-0 No. 45311 was departing with the 12.8pm Crewe-Llandudno, Ivatt 2-6-2T No. 41276 with the 12.45pm local to Rhyl while '43XX' 2-6-0 No. 7310 from Croes Newydd was backing empty stock into the station ready to work an afternoon local to Shrewsbury. No. 45311 had been transferred to Llandudno Junction in May 1962. No. 41276 was at Rhyl from new in October 1950 until December 1962 when it moved to the Southern Region at Brighton.

## CHAPTER 5 - CHESTER AND MOLD JUNCTION

### Approaching Chester General
### From the east

On a misty winter's day in early 1960 'Coronation' No. 46257 *City of Salford* has just passed under Station View bridge and is about to enter Chester General on the 9.20am Crewe-Holyhead, a regular running-in turn for engines newly outshopped from Crewe Works. After arrival at Holyhead the engine worked the 2.40pm passenger train to Bangor, the 5.40pm Bangor to Llandudno Junction and the 7.5pm Llandudno Junction to Holyhead. It returned to Crewe on the 6.35am Parcels (Horse and Carriage) the following morning. No. 46257 was at Carlisle Upperby from September 1958 until March 1961 and had AWS from August 1959. This picture was probably taken after a lengthy Non-Classified overhaul completed in February 1960. The last two 'Coronation' Pacifics, Nos 46256 and 46257 built under H.G. Ivatt, had a completely redesigned and simpler, rear frame arrangement to stiffen the hind end and eliminate fracturing of the rear spliced frames and to accommodate an improved type of ashpan. They had shorter 'chopped-off' cab side sheets and an improved arrangement of the reversing gear.

With the Chester No. 2 signal box, which together with No. 1 box controlled the east end of the station, towering in the background, BR Standard Class '2' 2-6-2T No. 84000 shunts Diagram 2125 LM&SR design horsebox No. M42546. The picture was taken near the end of No. 84000's time at Birkenhead Mollington Street where it left in June 1961 for Warrington Dallam. This British Railways design was based on the LM&SR Ivatt 2-6-2T with a boiler which was dimensionally almost the same as the LM&SR No. 7 boiler used on the Ivatt engines, but with a revised water delivery from a side clack valve arrangement rather than via a top feed. The most noticeable external difference was the sloping front footplate ahead of the cylinders, a retrograde step from the open arrangement of the LM&SR design. The Standard engines were all auto-fitted, weighed the same at 63tons 5cwt and had the same tractive effort as the later Ivatt engines.

**From the west and south**

The last of the Collett 'Grange' 4-6-0s until the new build No. 6880 is completed, No. 6879 *Overton Grange* in the cutting between the two short tunnels on the western approach to Chester General with the 8.10am SO Birmingham Snow Hill-Birkenhead in 1962. No. 6879 entered service in May 1939 and was at Tyseley from April 1960 until withdrawn in October 1965.

No. 7923 *Speke Hall* approaches Chester General with a Down express on 5th June 1962. One of the final batch of 'Modified Halls' built under British Railways' auspices and entering service in September 1950, it was allocated to Southall from October 1958 until October 1964. Although built with a Hawksworth tender it had the Collett type as pictured from March 1960 until withdrawal in June 1965. The pair of tracks on the left were the 'Shrewsbury & Chester', used by both Western Region trains to and from Saltney Junction and as the London Midland Region Slow lines to and from North Wales; those on the right were the 'Chester & Holyhead' or LMR Fast lines. Northgate Congregational Church is in the background and Victoria Road school is to its right.

CHAPTER 5 - CHESTER AND MOLD JUNCTION

Hughes-Fowler 'Crab' 2-6-0 No. 42886 leaves the 200 yards long Upper Northgate Street tunnel as it approaches Chester with a Saturday special from North Wales in July 1963. It was at Edge Hill from October 1962 until December 1964.

*Below*:
Stanier Class '5' No. 44986 with coal empties from Mold Junction about to pass through the shorter second tunnel beneath Victoria Road and Northgate station on the approach to Chester General on 1st June 1962. No. 44986 has one of the former coal-weighing tenders which it had been running with since 1946. It had been transferred from Warrington Dallam to Mold Junction in April 1962 but its stay there was short, and it left in November for Carlisle Kingmoor.

'Royal Scot' No. 46148 *The Manchester Regiment* with a Holyhead-London express on 27th July 1963. It spent its last two years working along the North Wales coast, at either Llandudno Junction or Holyhead, until withdrawn in November 1964. No. 46148 was the last to remain from a long line of the class at Holyhead and was looked after well by the shed staff and regarded as something of a 'pet' locomotive.

*Below:*
WD 'Austerity' 2-8-0 No. 90686 with a Class 'H' eastbound freight in 1962. It was built for the WD in December 1944 as No. 79225 and was allocated to Chester West shed from August 1948 until transferred to Gorton in April 1963. It is on the Up Fast line and has just passed through one of the two double-track bores which were under the main roads to Parkgate and Liverpool out of Chester.

Stanier '8F' 2-8-0 No. 48246 on an empty stock working, probably from Holyhead to Crewe, in the early 1960s during the time it was at Llandudno Junction between July 1961 and June 1964. This was regularly a long and heavy train, hence the use of an '8F'; this often happened with Llandudno Junction's Nos 48246 and 48771 'stretching their legs' rather than working their regular Penmaenmawr stone trains. The leading coach is a BR Mark 1 Kitchen/Buffet car, either a Diagram 20 or a Diagram 25. The Stanier '8F' design was selected for wartime production and modified for overseas operation by fitting Westinghouse air brakes, speed indicators, different couplings and injectors, steam heating, and handrails for shunters to ride on the steps. Their tyres were turned to a different profile to suit the European track. By the time the first engines were completed, France and the low countries were being overrun, and so there was no need for them to be sent there and the modifications were removed at Crewe Works to permit their use in Britain. No. 48246 was the first 2-8-0 built for the War Department, constructed by the North British Locomotive Company as WD No. 300 in May 1940. It was loaned to the LM&SR in September 1940 and given the number 8226. It went on loan to the GWR from October 1940 until September 1941 before returning to the War Department to be modified for overseas use and going to Persia. In 1948 the War Department offered British Railways the engines it still had in the Middle East and which were surplus to requirements. The ten engines which had been built in 1936/7 had their previous LM&SR identities restored but the eleven which had been built for the War Department were given new numbers. WD No. 70300, purchased in December 1949, became No. 48246 rather than No. 48226. It was the second '8F' to have the number 8246; the first was built for the War Department in 1940 and loaned to the LM&SR and subsequently returned from overseas to become No. 48774 in July 1957.

English Electric Type '4' No. D230 *Scythia* heads an Up parcels train in 1961. The first Type '4' was allocated to Holyhead for crew training in November 1959, and by the Spring of the following year the class became a regular sight on the North Wales Coast line on the mail trains, although it would be several years before they took over the other passenger work from steam. No. D230 became No. 40030 in 1974 under TOPS and was in service until 1983. Twenty-five of the London Midland Region's Type '4' diesels were named after ocean liners using the Port of Liverpool; their nameplates had a representation of the flag of each ship above the name with the name of its shipping line in smaller lettering underneath; No. D230 was named in Derby Works on 8th April 1961. *RMS Scythia* had entered service in 1921, one of a series of 19,000 ton 'intermediate' liners built by Cunard to operate in support of their large express liners for services between Liverpool and the US. It was requisitioned as a troop and supply ship during the Second World War and in 1950 *Scythia* became a passenger ship again, sailing from Britain to Canada and later to New York, working until 1958.

Edge Hill's 'Coronation' Pacific No. 46229 *Duchess of Hamilton* has passed under the second of the two bridges carrying the tracks into Northgate goods depot on 28th April 1962. It is probably working the Holyhead-Ordsall Lane 'Horse & Carriage' which was always well loaded and usually had Class '8' power. After withdrawal in February 1964 No. 46229 was purchased by Butlin's and was exhibited at their Minehead holiday camp until it was acquired in 1975 by the National Railway Museum, initially on loan and then purchased outright in 1987. After overcoming some difficult technical problems, 46229 was restored to running order in 1980 and it became the Museum's flagship locomotive until it needed repairs in 1985. When these were completed in 1989 it returned to the mainline for seven years until its boiler ticket expired in 1996. Its streamlined casing was restored at Tyseley Locomotive Works between 2005 and 2009 and *Duchess of Hamilton* is currently a static exhibit at York where it is in the same showroom condition as when it went to the United States World's Fair in 1939 in lieu of 6220 *Coronation*.

A '28XX' 2-8-0 waits on the avoiding line to gain access to the line to Saltney Junction and the south with a freight from the Wirral, as Ivatt Class '2' 2-6-2T No. 41244 passes under Chester No. 6 signal box as it approaches Chester with a Rhyl-Chester stopping train. No. 41244 was built in October 1949 and was at Wellingborough until August 1951 when it was transferred to Rhyl where it stayed until April 1955, moving to Rhosddu, the former Great Central Railway shed at Wrexham.

*J.D. Mills/Rail Archive Stephenson*

On the same day as the picture on the previous page and with the '28XX' on the right still waiting to cross the junction, 'Castle' Class 4-6-0 No. 5032 *Usk Castle* with an express from Paddington when it was paired with a Hawksworth straight-sided tender between May 1952 and August 1953. No. 5032 was a Stafford Road engine from November 1951 until March 1958 when it went to Newton Abbot. It hauled the first British Railways train to leave Paddington on 1st January 1948, the 12.5am to Birkenhead which it would have taken as far as Chester. The first two coaches of the train are ex-GWR 'Toplight' stock dating from the first decade of the century and still in top link service fifty years later. The 80-lever frame No. 6 box opened in 1903 had to be mounted on a gantry because of space restrictions and to ensure the signalmen had a good view of the lines at the west end of the triangular Chester South Junction. In the left background are wagons on one of the Northgate sidings and immediately behind No. 5032 is the side of Northgate engine shed.

*J.D. Mills/Rail Archive Stephenson*

Crewe South Stanier '8F' 2-8-0 No. 48256 with a train of engineers' ballast wagons, probably from the quarry at Penmaenmawr, runs in front of Chester No. 6 signal box. It is on the Up Main line and has passed through the tunnel and under the bridges which carried the tracks and sidings into Northgate. A set of coaches is standing on the line into the depot, the large gabled building behind the signal. The lines on the right were the third part of the triangle at the west end of General station, the through lines which allowed trains running between Saltney Junction and Birkenhead to avoid the station. No. 48256 was built by North British Locomotive Company for the War Department as No. 394 in September 1941 and was purchased by British Railways in October 1949 after serving overseas since October 1941. The first '8F' numbered 8256 was loaned to the LM&SR between November 1940 and July 1941 but did not return to Britain. This picture was taken after completion of a Heavy General repair in May 1960 but before its return to Crewe Works for AWS to be fitted a few weeks later. Note the star below the cab number indicating that the wheels had been re-balanced up to fifty percent of their reciprocating weight for fitted freight work.

Caprotti Class '5' 4-6-0 No. 44749 on a train from the North Wales coast in front of the large 176-lever frame Chester No. 4 signal box built in 1904. The twenty engines built in 1948 had the most fundamental changes to Stanier's original Class '5' design and were fitted with 'British Caprotti' rotary-cam poppet valve gear. Poppet-type valves, two inlet and two exhaust valves for each cylinder, were provided instead of the normal slide or piston valves and were mounted outside the exhaust valves at the fronts of the cylinders which meant that the steam pipes had to be extended further forward within the smokebox and passed through the cylinder wrappers slightly higher up than previously. On the engines fitted with roller bearings, of which No. 44749 was one, the steam pipes were cranked about a foot above the cylinders which had a disastrous effect on the front-end appearance. Almost half of the Caprottis were originally allocated to Longsight but in September 1960 the Manchester shed lost seven of them following the start of electric operation on the Manchester to Crewe line. Six went to Llandudno Junction including No. 44749 after brief spells elsewhere, increasing that shed's total to nine engines. It left for Speke Junction in November 1961 and was withdrawn in September 1964.

Green-liveried 'Western' diesel-hydraulic No. D1003 *Western Pioneer* is signalled into Platform 2 as it arrives at Chester General with the 1.10pm Paddington to Birkenhead in 1963. The train will reverse and be taken north by a London Midland Region engine, possibly the Fairburn 2-6-4T No. 42240 waiting on the right. No. D1003 was built at Swindon in April 1962 and No. 42240 had been transferred from Corkerhill to Chester Midland shed in February 1960. Note the two LM&SR horseboxes on the left which presumably will have brought their occupants to Chester racecourse.

Paddington-Birkenhead expresses were worked forward from Chester from the early 1950s by London Midland Region 2-6-4Ts. The number of enthusiasts with their heads out of every available carriage window and the blue and grey livery of the first coach shows this was right at the end of the through service. Stanier 2-6-4T No. 42616 passes in front of No. 4 box as arrives from Birkenhead on 4th March 1967. Its smokebox been adorned with painted straps and hinges for the occasion. No. 42616 had been transferred to Mollington Street from Carnforth in March 1966 and left for Low Moor in May 1967 but was withdrawn in September.

CHAPTER 5 - CHESTER AND MOLD JUNCTION

'Star' Class 4-6-0 No. 4053 *Princess Alexandra* from Wolverhampton Stafford Road arrives at Chester General with a train from Shrewsbury in 1952. It was built in June 1914, one of a batch of fifteen named after Princesses, and was withdrawn in July 1954. The GWR goods shed is immediately to the right of No. 4053 and on the extreme right a 'Prairie' tank and a Pannier tank are in the sidings alongside the GWR engine shed.

*J.D. Mills/Rail Archive Stephenson*

'Castle' No. 5038 *Morlais Castle* arriving with a parcels train is under the second of the two impressive L&NWR gantries at the west end of General station; the other by No. 4 signal box is in the background. No. 5038 had been allocated to Old Oak Common before moving to Shrewsbury in March 1958 and was there until May 1962 when it moved to Oxford and then to Reading from where it was withdrawn in September 1963.

By February 1964 Brush Type '4' diesel-electrics had taken over the Paddington-West Midlands trains from the 'Western' diesel-hydraulics. Although most trains continued to be steam hauled north of Shrewsbury and would remain so until through services from Paddington ended in March 1967, diesels worked some of the trains through to Chester. No. D1714 brings in the 1.10pm Paddington to Birkenhead later in that year, and is signalled into Platform 3. It was built at the Brush Traction Works in Loughborough in February 1964 and was allocated to Old Oak Common. It became No. 47124 in April 1974. Immediately to the right of the locomotive are two diesel multiple units outside the diesel depot which had been converted from the GWR engine shed in 1960.

One of the split headcode box English Electric Type '4' diesel-electrics, No. D334 arrives with the Up 'Irish Mail' in 1963. It is about to pass Chester No. 3A signal box which replaced an L&NWR box in 1959 at the end of the Up island platform (Nos 9, 10, 13 and 14); the former GWR Chester West Goods Depot is on the right. No. D334 was built at Vulcan Foundry in March 1961 and allocated to Crewe North, it was withdrawn as No. 40134 in 1981. 'The Irish Mail' dates back to August 1848 and was the first train in Britain to have an official name, although this was not carried on the roofboards until 1927; the name continued in use on ordinary passenger services long after the train conveyed the mails but was finally discontinued in 2002.

## Chester General station

After the L&NWR/GWR Joint station was modernised in 1890, it had three long through platforms each divided operationally into two platforms, Nos 4 and 5 on the Down side, Nos 9 and 10 on the Up side and Nos 13 and 14 which were bi-directional. At the east end there were three original bays, Nos 6, 7 and 8 supplemented by two new bays, Nos 11 and 12 between Platforms 10 and 13. The west end had three bays, Nos 1, 2 and 3, and most Western Region trains used Platforms 2 and 3 with a few reversing in the Up and Down through Platform 14. London Midland Region services used all of the other platforms with Nos 4 and 5 more intensively used than Nos 9 and 10 which shared Up through trains with Platform 13. Two pairs of scissors crossings connecting the platform lines to their respective adjacent Up and Down through lines enabled Platforms 4 and 5 and Platforms 9 and 10 to be occupied simultaneously since trains could arrive or depart independently.

General station and its approach lines were controlled by seven signal boxes, Nos 1 to 6 and 3A, with several impressive signal gantries at the west end of the station. The L&NWR signals survived until the late 1970s when they were replaced by colour lights and they were probably the last full set of lower quadrant signals to remain in use at a major station. The signal boxes were operational until May 1984 when a new power box was commissioned.

### 1950s

'Britannia' 4-6-2 No. 70046 waits to depart from Chester General with a Down express in the mid-1950s. It was one of five of the class which went from new to Holyhead in 1954 and was there until November 1959. No. 70046 was the last but one of the class to be named, becoming *Anzac* in September 1959. This was the abbreviation for the Australian and New Zealand Army Corps formed in Egypt in December 1914 and operated during the Gallipoli campaign. The Corps was disbanded in 1916 but was briefly re-formed during the Second World War.

In late 1952, Old Oak Common lost all its 'County' Class 4-6-0s, seven to Laira and five to Chester where they replaced the 'Castles' on the Birkenhead-London trains between Chester and Wolverhampton. No. 1017 *County of Hereford* after arrival in Platform 13/14 rather than in one of the bays on 6th April 1957. It was allocated to Wolverhampton Stafford Road between May 1955 and December 1960 and was not fitted with a double chimney until March 1959. The former L&NWR goods depot is in the background.

Fowler '2P' 4-4-0 No. 40653 at Chester General after arrival in Platform 5 during 1957. This was one of the LM&SR-built engines which only entered service a few months before William Stanier took over as CME in January 1932. They incorporated minor modifications to the 1912 Midland Railway design to allow wider route availability. Also, the driving wheel diameter was reduced from 7ft 0½in. to 6ft 9in. and the boiler pressure was increased from 160lbs per sq. inch to 180lbs. No. 40653 was transferred from Northampton to Crewe North in March 1957 but remained then mainly in store until withdrawn in November 1959.

In the foreground of the lower picture is one of the scissors crossings, this one allowing independent use of the two ends of the long platform, numbered 9 at the west end and 10 at the east end. The crossings were controlled by the pairs of signals, as in front of No. 40653. Note the Scottish Region coach at the front of the train.

*Kenneth Field/Rail Archive Stephenson*

## 1960s

'Royal Scot' 4-6-0 No. 46156 *The South Wales Borderer* runs in with a Down stopping train which will use one of the scissors crossovers to gain access to Platform 4. It was one of the final batch of twenty of the class built at Derby in 1930 and had been converted with a taper boiler as late as May 1954. The picture was taken while it was allocated to Holyhead, from June 1960 onwards, and before March 1961 when it was fitted with a Smith-Stone speed indicator. No. 46156 has passed under the footbridge at the east end of the station from which the picture below and on the following page were taken.
*Kenneth Field/Rail Archive Stephenson*

'Coronation' No. 46254 *City of Stoke-on-Trent* waits on the Up Main for the signal before departing towards Crewe in 1962. A 2-6-4T is at the end of Platform 10, probably on its way to Midland shed and a Stanier Class '5' is behind it in bay Platform 11.

*City of Stoke-on-Trent* was one of four London Midland Region Pacifics loaned to the Western Region in early 1956 when the Western's Kings were found to have fractures to their bogie frames, resulting in all of the class being stopped for examination and then taken out of service while their bogie frames were welded. No. 46254 worked WR expresses between Paddington and Wolverhampton and also the 'Cornish Riviera'.

As part of the limited modernisation of the station in 1961, new 'lozenge'-shaped fluorescent tubular lamps inscribed with the station name replaced the metal totem signs.

The east end of Chester General Station on 4th August 1962 as the crew of LM&SR '3F' 0-6-0T No. 47297 chat with an enthusiast at the end of Platform 5. It has lamps above each buffer signifying that it is on station pilot duties. Platform 10 is on the left. On the Up Main Churchward '43XX' 2-6-0 No. 5399, having backed through is signalled to take the Crewe line on its way to Chester Midland shed. According to the RCTS Traffic Survey carried out on this day No. 5399 later took over the 5.07pm from Birkenhead to Barmouth from 2-6-4T No. 42493. No. 5399 was a former resident of Chester West shed and moved to Croes Newydd after that shed closed to steam in April 1960, but by this date it had only six weeks left in service. In the left distance is the tall, 182-lever Chester No. 2 Signal Box that controlled the east end of the station and remained in use until 1979. The lines to the right are the Whitchurch/Crewe bays. The circular tower in the distance is the 84 feet high water tower at the Boughton Water Pumping Station alongside the Shropshire Union Canal which was built in 1853 and extended to its present height in 1884 for the Chester Waterworks Company and was given Grade II Listing in 2006. Note the railwayman walking on the wooden walkway over the point rodding; these were used at most large L&NWR stations.

The RCTS Survey on Saturday 4th August 1962 records that BR Standard Class '4' 2-6-0 No. 76089 had taken the 7.8am Wigan to Llandudno train which arrived punctually at Llandudno Junction. In this picture No. 76089 has returned with the 11.50am Llandudno to Manchester Victoria which reached Chester General twelve minutes late. On the centre left is Derby 'Twin' Motor Brake Second No. M 50965 and beyond a Stanier Class '5' 4-6-0 is moving off. Ahead is the unusually tall Chester No. 2 Box which operated the ex-L&NWR lower-quadrant signals. There are five water columns, a small platelayer's hut or fogman's hut and a larger brick-built structure. Note 'Broken Glass – Take Care' chalked on the parcels van No. M 31362 M behind No. 76089.

Three engines are rather excessive for a short parcels train so we can only assume that two of them were working back home to avoid light engine movements. Crewe North's No. 70051 *Firth of Forth* and a second 'Britannia' top-and-tail a Stanier Class '5' 4-6-0 as they wait in the Up Main or through road. No. 70051 was a former Scottish Region engine, originally at Polmadie before moving to Corkerhill in April 1962 and then to Crewe North in November 1962.

A Class 'E' Down freight headed by Stanier '8F' 2-8-0 No. 48344 passes through Chester General on 16th September 1965. It had been allocated to Trafford Park since April 1959 and was in service until March 1968.

The ice-cream vendor standing by the first coach has finished selling his wares to the passengers of a Derby-Llandudno Summer Saturday holiday express and Hughes/Fowler 2-6-0 No. 42769 is ready to depart from Platform 4 on 22nd July 1961. The 'Crab' which had been at Burton shed since July 1960 was built as LM&SR No. 13079 in July 1927 and was withdrawn in February 1964. Note the vintage workmen's dumper truck in the foreground and the builders working halfway down the platform with their mobile compressor left in the middle of the platform. The overall roof has already been removed.

There is a lot more activity later in the day on Platform 4 as what looks like a wedding party crowds around the third coach of the relief express from Euston to Holyhead hauled by 'Princess Royal' 4-6-2 No. 46209 *Princess Beatrice*. The young trainspotters clearly have more interest in the Pacific than the 'Crab'. No. 46209 had been transferred to Crewe North in September 1960 and would go into store there six weeks later; it emerged at the end of January 1962 but was withdrawn that September.

Caprotti Class '5' 4-6-0 No. 44687 on 28th August 1961 at the west end of Platform 13 which together with Platform 14 formed a bi-directional through road. Beyond Platform 9 on the right was Platform 10, the through platforms used by most of the trains to either Crewe or Manchester originating from the North Wales coast. Above left is the small, 36-lever No. 3 signal box which controlled the scissors crossovers at the centre of the Up and Down Main through platforms; the signs direct passengers to bay Platforms 11 and 12, at the east end of the station.

No. 44687 was the final LM&SR Class '5' of the 842 engines built under Stanier and Ivatt. Together with No. 44686, it incorporated both the post-war modifications introduced by Ivatt and a double chimney but also an improved version of the Caprotti valve gear to remedy problems experienced with the first twenty Caprottis with poor accessibility of the inside drive-line and a tendency for the valves to stick open if the engine primed. The pair were allocated to Longsight when new in 1951 staying there until 1960 when they moved to Llandudno Junction; they were considered by crews and observers to be equivalent to a Class '6' engine.

The final two Class '5' 4-6-0s were not the only Stanier design to be modified by George Ivatt, the final pair of 'Coronation' 4-6-2s also incorporated several important modifications. He had already introduced a number of features on the post-war Class '5' 4-6-0s, such as self-cleaning smokeboxes, hopper ashpans and rocking grates, and these had been applied to 'Coronation' Nos 6253-6255. The aim was to increase the mileage between repairs for the passenger engines to 100,000 miles per annum and reduce the time on servicing and maintenance. In addition to these three improvements, the final two 4-6-2s were to have roller bearings, manganese steel axlebox liners and larger superheaters. Crimson lake liveried No. 46256 *Sir William A. Stanier F.R.S.*, standing at the west end of Platform 4 with the 1D16 from Crewe to Holyhead which was the regular running-in turn from Crewe North, was considered by many to be the 'ultimate' Pacific; for some reason No. 46257 had a less favourable reputation; it was always allocated to Crewe North from new in December 1947 except for a few weeks away in late 1959/early 1960. The partially enclosed footbridge leading to Hoole Road and the rear of No. 3A box are to its left.

'County' No. 1019 *County of Merioneth* simmers gently in Platform 2 while its driver returns with a brew. It has an 89A shed plate but was only at Shrewsbury for its last four months in service before withdrawal in February 1963. The umbrella-type roofing was fitted in around 1961, and at the same time platform edges and copings were renewed and the level slightly raised.

An example of the wide variety of classes which the spotter could see at Chester on a summer Saturday, L&NER 'B1' 4-6-0 No. 61085 passes through non-stop with a train to the North Wales coast. It appears to be running wrong line on the Up through line although it is heading west, possibly due to Sunday engineering work. The picture was taken when No. 61085 was allocated to Woodford Halse, between November 1959 and October 1960.

*Kenneth Field/Rail Archive Stephenson*

The 'Britannia' with the longest name and very large, red-backed nameplates, *The Territorial Army 1908-1958*, which it received in July 1958 waits in Platform 5 with a Down express in 1963. No. 70048 had been transferred to Willesden in October 1962 and was there until the end of that year. The lowering of top lamp brackets was not introduced until early 1963 so it appears that its new shed at Holyhead had not replaced the 1A shed plate. One of the scissors crossovers allowing use of the two ends of the platform, Nos 9 and 10, with the Up through road is on the left.

'Britannia' 4-6-2 No. 70045 *Lord Rowallan* in late 1963 with Chester No. 3A signal box in the background; this box was only built in late 1959 at the west end of the Up island platform (Nos 14 and 9). No. 70045 was the first of the second batch of 'Britannia' Pacifics which went new to Holyhead in 1954. In July 1957 it was named *Lord Rowallan* in honour of the man who became Chief Scout in 1945 after a distinguished military career. No. 70045 moved away in December 1959 but returned three years later and was at Holyhead until June 1965. The footbridge in the background extended right across the west end of the station and led to Hoole Road, providing a short-cut to or from the north side. It caught fire in in the late 1950s leading to the removal of part of the covering and it remained in this condition until it was demolished in 1969.

## 1970s

By now a Class '24', BR Sulzer Type '2' No. 5041 was still in green livery, albeit with full yellow ends, no 'D'-prefix and still with hand/footholds. It went from new to Ipswich in September 1959 and moved to the London Midland Region in August 1967 to the Stoke Division (D05), based at Crewe. It became No. 24041 in September 1973 and was withdrawn in July 1976.

Chester was the scene of a violent and destructive incident in the early hours of 9th July 1969 when the 02.25 Birkenhead - Etruria iron ore train, weighing approximately 1,000 tons and hauled by Class '47' No. 1617 was reported out of control and diverted into the diesel depot to avoid the station area. Two locomotives and eleven wagons were derailed, with Class '24' Nos. 5031/43/93 and 5138/39 extensively damaged and four of them were withdrawn the following month.

Three years later there was a second incident involving Class '24's at Chester when No. 5028 hauling an Ellesmere Port-Mold Junction freight in May 1972 ran away and was diverted into bay Platform 11 where it collided with a DMU. The first two wagons contained gas oil for the diesel depot and caught fire destroying the locomotive, six DMU vehicles, part of the overall roof and severely damaging the refreshment room.

The English Electric Type '4' diesel-electrics took over not only the express passenger work on the North Wales main line but were also used on the heavier freight duties Now in rail blue with full yellow ends, Class '40' No. 314 on the Up through line with a train of Diagram 1/167 HKV Iron Ore hoppers on 20th September 1973. It was withdrawn from Healey Mills in October 1980 as No. 40114.

## Freight and parcels

Both the L&NWR and the GWR had large goods depots on the north side of the station which freight trains accessed from the Up and Down Goods lines. Stanier '8F' 2-8-0 No. 48101 shunting its train back, in very unlike '8F' condition shortly after a Light Intermediate overhaul completed in March 1961, was at Saltley from February 1959 until March 1964. It has a star below the cab number indicating that the wheels had been re-balanced up to fifty percent of their reciprocating weight for fitted freight work although here it is on a Class 'F' express unfitted freight, probably from Warrington to Birkenhead. On the left is a nice example of a L&NWR bracket signal with small subsidiary arms.

At the head of a very lengthy Up 'Horse and Carriage', the 12.10pm Holyhead-Ordsall Lane, Crewe North 'Coronation' No. 46254 *City of Stoke-on-Trent* is on the Up Main and no doubt some stock would be attached/detached. The term 'Horse and Carriage' is folklore amongst railwaymen in North Wales and always referred to the midday parcels vans/ECS working from Holyhead picking up at Bangor, Llandudno Junction and Chester. This train always loaded heavy and was a favourite for a 'Coronation' in their twilight years. The service returned parcels and vans which had arrived overnight in North Wales on mail, parcels and newspaper traffic, not only for Welsh towns but also for Ireland.

By 1963, 'Coronations' displaced from their WCML express duties were appearing on the heavy cattle and insulated meat traffic from Holyhead to York but mostly to London Broad Street. No. 46228 *Duchess of Rutland* waits on the Up Slow at Chester General on 30th July 1963. It was at Crewe North from June 1959, a year after it was repainted in LM&SR style crimson lake. In the background to the left of the water tower is the L&NWR goods shed and parcels depot.

'Royal Scot' No. 46148 *The Manchester Regiment* with the Holyhead-Broad Street meat train. There were two trains on weekdays, 4A18 and 4A21 leaving Holyhead at 4.10pm and 4.40pm respectively. No. 46148 spent its last two years working along the North Wales coast, at either Llandudno Junction or Holyhead, until withdrawn in November 1964. The L&NWR goods yard is on the right.

A Down freight bypasses the station using the Down Goods line on its way to Mold Junction headed by Ivatt Class '4' 2-6-0 No. 43052, probably in 1963. It was the third of the class built at Doncaster in August 1950 for the North Eastern Region, and was initially at Scarborough then Selby until May 1959 when it was transferred to the LMR; it was at Crewe South from October 1962 until withdrawn in November 1966. Chester 3A signal box is on the right and the large parcels depot on the left with a Scammell Scarab 'Mechanical Horse' with its distinctive three-wheeled tractor which featured automatic coupling and uncoupling of the trailer. These were produced until 1967 and BR had a large fleet of them, all painted originally in crimson and cream livery.

A very unexpected 'cop' for the local 'spotters, Carlisle Kingmoor's 'Clan' 4-6-2 No. 72005 *Clan Macgregor* passes through the station with a freight to Mold Junction on 29th August 1964. The five Kingmoor based engines in the class worked the Glasgow to Manchester expresses in the early 1960s and No. 72005 had probably been appropriated for this freight turn by Patricroft shed as a fill-in before it returned north.

## Departing from Chester General
### East

Carlisle Upperby 'Coronation' 4-6-2 No. 46221 *Queen Elizabeth* sets off towards Crewe with just four coaches behind and carrying Class 'C' lamps indicating a parcels or Empty Coaching Stock train. It is passing Chester No. 1, a non-descript BR mechanical 60-lever box, which replaced the 1890 L&NWR cabin in 1958 and controlled the junction between the Crewe and Helsby/Warrington lines with the latter passing immediately in front of the box; Chester No. 2 box is visible in the distance beyond the road bridge.

In crimson lake with LM&SR-style lining 'Coronation' 46248 *City of Leeds* with a Holyhead-London express has gone under Hoole Lane bridge on 7th June 1962. It is about to pass Chester Midland shed with the Helsby/Warrington line behind the embankment on the right. No. 46248 was at Crewe North from September 1960 until withdrawal in 1964.

## West

LM&SR Fowler '2P' 4-4-0 No. 40675 leaves Chester General with the 2.25pm slow to Rhyl in 1952, with the rear coaches passing underneath Hoole Road. It was built in February 1932 and was allocated to Rhyl between May 1948 and November 1955 when it moved to Chester Midland shed.

*J.D. Mills/Rail Archive Stephenson*

Unnamed 'Patriot' 4-6-0 No. 45513 sets off with a North Wales express, probably in 1952. It had been transferred from Preston to Crewe North in January 1950 and was there until 1955.

*J.D. Mills/Rail Archive Stephenson*

The Great Western introduced the '64XX' class of panniers in 1932 to replace the steam railmotors and ancient auto-fitted engines on branch passenger trains. They had the same 4ft 7½in. driving wheels as the '57xx' class and were intended for use on the more steeply graded lines whereas their compatriots, the '54XX' had 5ft 2in. wheels; they had a 180 lbs per sq. in. boiler pressure which gave them a tractive effort of only 18,010 lbs compared with the 22,515 lbs of the '57XX'. In a photograph taken from the steps of No. 6 signal box No. 6405 leaves Chester probably on a Llangollen/Bala line service with a pair of auto trailers, Nos.78 and 40, in 1952. It was allocated to Croes Newydd from July 1948 until withdrawn in June 1959. The engine in the background, a 'Castle', is on the turntable of the GWR shed.
*J.D. Mills/Rail Archive Stephenson*

CHAPTER 5 - CHESTER AND MOLD JUNCTION

Hawksworth 'Modified Hall' 4-6-0 No. 7922 *Salford Hall* sets off with an express to Paddington in the early 1960s. Although built with a flat-sided tender it was paired with a Collett tender between March 1960 and November 1963 and was at Shrewsbury from September 1958, although in store there until June 1959. Note on the right of the picture the two 'County' Class 4-6-0s waiting to take over the next Western Region departures.

A very clean 'Crab' 2-6-0 with Empty Coaching Stock for Birkenhead, probably taken shortly after completion of its last Heavy General repair in November 1961. No. 42936 was one of the final batch of ten built at Crewe in late 1932 after William Stanier had taken over as the LM&SR Chief Mechanical Engineer. It had been fitted with AWS in October 1959, transferred to Birkenhead in November 1960 and was withdrawn from there in July 1965.

'Royal Scot' 4-6-0 No. 46156 *The South Wales Borderer* departs with a Down express in the early 1960s, as one of Chester's three LM&SR '3F' 0-6-0Ts shunts in the adjacent sidings with an unidentified 'Jubilee' to its right. The picture was taken while it was allocated to Holyhead from June 1960 onwards and after March 1961 when it was fitted with a Smith-Stone speed indicator. It was transferred to Camden in March 1963 but returned to Holyhead the following month before leaving for Willesden in June 1963 and moved on again four months later to end its days at Annesley on the former Great Central until withdrawn in October 1964.

CHAPTER 5 - CHESTER AND MOLD JUNCTION

The spindly ironwork that supported Chester No. 6 signal box because of the restricted space is evident as 'Castle' No. 4083 *Abbotsbury Castle* leaves Chester with an express to Paddington in early 1952. It moved from Shrewsbury to Wolverhampton Stafford Road in November 1950 and had a Collett 4,000 gallon tender from August 1951, replacing the Hawksworth pattern which it ran with from October 1946. The first coach is a GWR 'Toplight' All-Third.
*J.D. Mills/Rail Archive Stephenson*

'Jubilee' 4-6-0 No. 45671 *Prince Rupert* with a Class 'E' freight to Mold Junction in June 1962 bursts out of the 106 yards long Victoria Road/Windmill Lane Tunnel above which were the platforms of Northgate station. This was the first of the tunnels out of General station, and No. 45671 is about to enter the second one, Upper Northgate Street Tunnel. No. 45671 was at Warrington Dallam from October 1961 until withdrawn in November 1963.

The East Midlands sheds regularly used their '9F' 2-10-0s for Summer Saturday excursion work in 1962 and 1963. This picture was taken after No. 92089 had been transferred from Annesley to Leicester Midland in February 1963. It was there until September 1964 when it moved to Speke Junction and was one of many of the class that ended its days at Birkenhead from where it was withdrawn in February 1967. Unlike the Upper Northgate Street tunnel which had twin bores, the Victoria Road/Windmill Lane tunnel had a single bore spanning all four tracks.

The 2,700 bhp 'Western' diesel-hydraulics were introduced on the Paddington-Birkenhead services at the start of the 1962 Winter Timetable. They were put on complex two-day diagrams from Laira, covering a 700-mile round trip Plymouth-London-Wolverhampton-London-Plymouth and these were soon extended into three-day turns that included working onwards from Wolverhampton to Chester. No. D1020 *Western Hero* with the 8.55am Birkenhead - Paddington soon after it came into service in May 1963 will have taken over the train at Chester from a London Midland 2-6-4T. Brush Type '4's started to arrive at Old Oak Common for crew training in October 1963 in preparation for taking over the Paddington-Wolverhampton expresses – this was at the instigation of the LMR who had taken over responsibility for the line north of Banbury and did not want the hydraulics working into their territory. By February 1964 they had all but ousted the 'Western's north of Birmingham. Note the two circular banner repeater signals with the Up Fast off and the Up Slow on.

# CHAPTER 5 - CHESTER AND MOLD JUNCTION

## Crossing the Canal

Unnamed 'Patriot' No. 45544 crosses over the Shropshire Union Canal with a London-North Wales train on 10th April 1954 with the start of the Northgate flight of locks on the right of the picture. This was one of the final ten 'Patriot' 4-6-0s and was not built until March 1934, over two years after Stanier became CME of the LM&SR; unlike the earlier members of the class these were officially new engines and had Stanier-pattern wheels with triangular section rims and tyres secured by Gibson rings. No. 45544 was at Crewe North from September 1952 until January 1955.

'Royal Scot' 4-6-0 No. 46116 *Irish Guardsman* on the canal bridge and about to pass beneath the City walls with the 4.32pm Down Ordinary Passenger to Llandudno on 5th May 1956. It was on loan to Holyhead from Carlisle Upperby which lasted less than two months. Note how little traffic there is on the road in this and the picture above.

The Western Region trains used the pair of tracks on the right between Chester General and Saltney Junction. The rear of the train hauled by Shrewsbury's 'Manor' Class 4-6-0 No. 7812 *Erlestoke Manor* is under the bridge at the end of Canal Street, having just come through the pair of tunnels beneath the main road to Liverpool and the Wirral, and Victoria Street. *Erlestoke Manor* – which is now preserved and based at the Severn Valley Railway having been rescued from Woodham's scrapyard at Barry – had been transferred from Truro to Shrewsbury in October 1960; it moved to Croes Newydd in November 1961.

Four Derby 'Lightweight' DMUs work in multiple on a special to Llandudno heading out of Chester in the late-1950s. After it passes beneath the city's walls it will head out over the viaduct alongside the Roodee. The spire in the right background belongs to St. John's Church.
*Kenneth Field/Rail Archive Stephenson*

Fowler '2P' 4-4-0 No. 40679 heads out of Chester and has crossed over the tall embankment overlooking the picturesque Water Tower Gardens with a Down 'Ordinary Passenger' train in 1952. Built at Derby in March 1932 it is in early BR livery with 10in. LM&SR block style stock numbers and 8in. tender lettering. It has a 6K shedplate which was the code for Rhyl from February 1952 onwards; it was there from October 1951 until December 1955 when it was transferred to Chester Midland. *J.D. Mills/Rail Archive Stephenson*

LM&SR 'Compound' 4-4-0 No. 40925, built by Vulcan Foundry in May 1927, heads towards Saltney Junction with an express for the North Wales coast in 1952. It has a 6G shed plate, Llandudno Junction's code from February 1952, and was there until June 1957. At this date the majority of the North Wales expresses were still worked by the 4-4-0s although they would soon be displaced by 4-6-0s. *J. D. Mills/Rail Archive Stephenson*

**At the Roodee**

Father and son watch BR Standard Class '5' 4-6-0 No. 73071 as it heads out of Chester across the Dee over the three 100ft span bridge with a Down North Wales express. It went new to Chester Midland in November 1954 and was there until May 1963, except for fifteen months on loan to Kings Cross 'Top Shed' in 1956/7 for use in testing of British Railways AWS, which was being developed from the LM&SR Hudd system at Doncaster Works. Two locomotives, No. 73071 and Stanier Class '5' No. 44911, were loaned from Chester to take part in the early trials of the new system. They appeared on outer suburban work and Cambridge turns and were tested on the prototype AWS section from New Barnet to Huntingdon. The pair of lines nearer the gasworks have long since been abandoned, even though they ran over the newer of the two bridges. On the right of the picture is the Roodee, Chester's racecourse, which has several claims to fame in horse racing history. The first recorded prize given to the winner of a horse race, a hand painted wooden bowl, was presented to the winner of a race at Chester in 1512. Henry Gee, who became mayor of Chester in 1539, introduced an annual horse race meeting on the Roodee which makes Chester Racecourse the oldest continuous site of horse racing in the British Isles. The term 'gee-gee' apparently derives from the important part played by Henry Gee in the development of the horse racing sport.

*Kenneth Field/Rail Archive Stephenson*

'Castle' Class 4-6-0 No. 5031 *Totnes Castle* crosses the River Dee as it leaves Chester with an express to Paddington in the mid-1950s before it was fitted with a double chimney in June 1959. Except for a few weeks at Chester in 1955, it was at Stafford Road shed from new in May 1934 until the Wolverhampton shed closed in September 1963; *Totnes Castle* was withdrawn from Oxley six weeks later. *Kenneth Field/Rail Archive Stephenson*

With the Roodee racecourse in the background, '9F' 2-10-0 No. 92045 on its way to Mold Junction passes an English Electric Class '40' on a train of blue/grey Mark 1s from North Wales on 4th March 1967. No. 92045 was one of three '9F' 2-10-0s transferred from Wellingborough to Bidston in 1956 to work the John Summers iron ore trains. They moved to Birkenhead Mollington Street which took over the iron ore trains when Bidston shed was closed in February 1963. No. 92045 was withdrawn in September 1967. Chester Racecourse is now officially recognised by the *Guinness Book of World Records* as the oldest racecourse in the world and is still in operation today.

### Mold Junction engine shed

Mold Junction, where the Mold & Denbigh line left the Chester & Holyhead line, was the principal freight marshalling yard for North Wales coast traffic with a large engine shed opened by the L&NWR in 1890 to serve the extensive freight yards. The allocation in the 1950s comprised freight and mixed traffic engines; in 1950 seventeen '8F' 2-8-0s, four '4F' 0-6-0s, seven Class '5' 4-6-0s and four Stanier 2-6-0s and six '3F' 0-6-0Ts. By 1954 the mix had changed slightly as ten WD 'Austerity' 2-8-0s and three more '4F' 0-6-0s arrived, reducing the '8F' 2-8-0s to five, the Stanier 2-6-0s increased to eight plus two 'Crab' 2-6-0s offsetting the fall in Class '5' 4-6-0s to four; the same six '3F' 0-6-0Ts remained. The shed was coded 6B from 1935 onwards and was closed in April 1966. Its northlight roof was in poor condition by the end of the war but was not re-roofed until 1948/9.

A mix of LM&SR, GWR and BR Standard 4-6-0s at Mold Junction on 20th August 1961. Stanier Class '5' No. 45072 was on Mold Junction's books from September 1960 until November 1962 when it went to Carlisle Upperby. Collett 'Grange' No. 6841 *Marlas Grange* was from Bristol St. Philip's Marsh and a long way from home. Western Region engines were regular visitors to Mold Junction after Chester West shed closed in 1960.

LM&SR types dominate in 1965 with Stanier Class '5' 4-6-0 No. 45275 in the foreground. It had been at Mold Junction since 1942 except for a few months at Chester Midland in 1945 and did not leave until the shed closed in April 1966. To its left, Vulcan Foundry-built '8F' 2-8-0 No. 48090 did not arrive at the shed until January 1963 and also stayed until April 1966. '3F' 0-6-0T No. 47673 on the right had been transferred to Chester Midland shed from Longsight in April 1960 and moved to Llandudno Junction in May 1965.

BR Standard Class '5' 4-6-0 No. 73034 was a Shrewsbury engine, from 1958 until April 1966. Like No. 45275 in the picture above, its top lamp bracket has been moved down into the middle of the smokebox to remove the danger to footplatemen from working near high-voltage overhead wires. Note the Scottish Region painted Class '5' No. 45042 with large 10in. cab numbers with the rarely used '5MT' power classification alongside.

## Chester Midland engine shed

The former L&NWR shed opened in 1870 was an eight-road straight building and had around forty engines on its allocation in the 1950s. It supplied engines for the semi-fast services to North Wales and Manchester, usually '2P' and 'Compound' 4-4-0s, 2-6-4Ts for the local services, Stanier and later BR Standard Class '5' 4-6-0s for mixed-traffic work and '3F' 0-6-0Ts for shunting. In November 1950 it had two '2P' 4-4-0s, thirteen 'Compound' 4-4-0s, ten 2-6-4Ts, seven Class '5' 4-6-0s and seven '3F' 0-6-0Ts. There was little change over the next four years with two '2P' 4-4-0s, eleven 'Compound' 4-4-0s, eleven 2-6-4Ts, six Stanier Class '5' and three BR Standard Class '5' 4-6-0s and seven '3F' 0-6-0Ts in January 1954.

The GWR engines were transferred from Chester West in April 1960 when that shed was closed and it serviced the Western Region engines from that date. The shed was known as Chester Midland despite being a former L&NWR shed; it was coded 6A from 1935 onwards and closed on 5th June 1967.

Two of the long-standing Chester Midland Class '3F' 0-6-0Ts No. 47297 and No. 47375 at the shed on 24th March 1957. No. 47297 was there from new in October 1924 until withdrawn in June 1964. It was built by Hunslet Engineering Co. Ltd at Leeds as LM&SR No. 7137 and was renumbered to 7297 in 1935. North British Locomotive Company Glasgow-built No. 47375 was originally LM&SR No. 16458 and was at Chester from December 1947 until June 1961 when it moved to Carnforth.

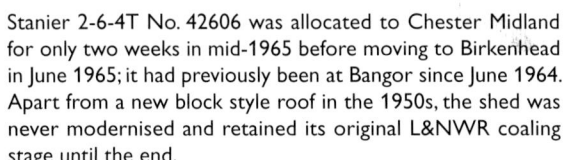

Stanier 2-6-4T No. 42606 was allocated to Chester Midland for only two weeks in mid-1965 before moving to Birkenhead in June 1965; it had previously been at Bangor since June 1964. Apart from a new block style roof in the 1950s, the shed was never modernised and retained its original L&NWR coaling stage until the end.

WD 'Austerity' 2-8-0 No. 90620, in typical scruffy lime-scaled condition, was a long way from its home shed of Wakefield on 19th April 1965. The BR Standard Class '4' 2-6-0 is no better and has lost its smokebox numberplate.

## Chester West engine shed

The former GWR shed consisted of two three-road buildings separated by four through roads, one of which had been owned by the L&NWR before it opened its own shed in 1870. The original GWR ex-Chester & Birkenhead Railway shed was modernised in 1928 and in 1957 it was re-roofed. At nationalisation the shed had fifty-one engines on its allocation ranging from fourteen 4-6-0s – one 'Castle', one 'Star', five 'Saint', six 'Hall' and one 'Grange'. For freight work it had five 2-8-0s, three '28XX' and two WD 'Austerity', three '56XX' 0-6-2Ts, ten 2-6-0s of which one was an 'Aberdare' and the remainder '43XX', one '2251' 0-6-0 and one 'Dean Goods'. There were seven '5101' 2-6-2Ts for local passenger work and nine '57XX' Panniers. In the intervening years, several Hawksworth 'County' 4-6-0s arrived and replaced some of the 'Castle' workings on the Paddington trains.

Ten years later, in February 1958 the shed was transferred to the London Midland Region and its 84K shed code was exchanged with Rhosddu's 6E as the Wrexham shed moved under Western Region control. The allocation at this date, all of which transferred to LMR stock, was three 'Castle' and three 'County' 4-6-0s, one 'Grange', six 'Hall' and five 'Manor' 4-6-0s, two '43XX' 2-6-0s, twelve '28XX' 2-8-0s, eight '5101' 2-6-2Ts and eleven '57XX' 0-6-0PTs; four BR Standard Class '5' 4-6-0s and two 'Austerity' 2-8-0s. The Grange and all of the Castles and Counties were transferred away three months later to be replaced by three more Standard Class '5' and three 'Jubilee' 4-6-0s, the latter only stayed until April 1959.

The shed was closed on 9th April 1960 and all its engines were transferred to Chester Midland. It was converted into a diesel depot to service the fleet of multiple units which arrived in early 1961.

The shed's solitary 'Dean Goods' 0-6-0 No. 2513 in 1952. It was at Chester from April 1947 until the end of 1954 when it was transferred to Brecon. Note the storm sheet has been opened out to cover the gap between the rear of the cab roof and the front of the tender.

Three locomotives of the several outside the new part of the former GWR shed to the west of Chester Midland station can be identified in this picture. In the centre, the '28XX' 2-8-0 was the one selected for preservation in the National Collection, the 1905-built No. 2818, which was at Ebbw Junction from October 1959 until May 1963. It was transferred from the National Railway Museum in 2017 to the STEAM Museum at Swindon. On either side of the 2-8-0, both BR Standard Class '5' 4-6-0 No. 73014 and Class '3' 2-6-2T No. 82001 were transferred to Chester West in the summer of 1958 and were there until April 1960 when they moved to Chester Midland. Note the date of the modernisation –1957 – recorded on the brickwork above the entrance.

Churchward '43XX' 2-6-0 No. 6306 is standing in one of the sidings off the turntable for the GWR shed which was within the triangle at the west end of Chester General station. It was allocated to Croes Newydd between June 1960 and withdrawal in November 1961. Chester No. 5 signal box which was on the Birkenhead line where the avoiding line from No. 6 box joined is in the left background. It differed from the other L&NWR pattern boxes at Chester having been built by a contractor for the Birkenhead Joint line in 1875 and with a hipped rather than a pitched roof.

'Castle' No. 5014 *Goodrich Castle* is also in the triangle with No. 1017 *County of Hereford* about to move onto the turntable in the background. This picture was taken during the short period in 1962 when No. 5014 had a Collett tender, from March to September, reverting to a Hawksworth type until withdrawn in February 1965. It had been at Old Oak Common since 1942 but moved to Tyseley in June 1964. The DMU depot which took over part of the former GWR shed is in the background.

The turntable was rarely used to actually turn engines, crews instead preferring the easier option of using the triangle.

Hawksworth 'County' 4-6-0 No. 1008 *County of Cardigan* backs away from the triangle towards the station in mid-1963. It had been fitted with a double chimney in March 1959. Although the first of the class, No. 1000 *County of Middlesex* had been built with a double blastpipe, it was not until mid-1956 that any of the others were modified. No. 1008 had been allocated to Chester West for six years up to August 1958 when it was transferred to Laira but came back north to Shrewsbury in February 1963, staying until September and was withdrawn a month later.

Churchward '43XX' 2-6-0 No. 7310 from Croes Newydd in passenger lined green livery waits near the turntable, probably in 1962. It was at the Wrexham shed from March 1947 until November 1963 when it was transferred to Severn Tunnel Junction.

No. 7310 was built in December 1921 using parts supplied by Robert Stephenson & Co. Ltd, who had been given an order for fifty of the class but only built thirty-five themselves, the other fifteen being erected in Swindon Works. Outside steam pipes were not fitted until September 1949.

The large amount of exposed pipework on BR Standard engines which was hidden away on pre-nationalisation designs shows up well in this picture of No. 72006 *Clan MacKenzie* taken by Jim Carter from No. 6 Signal Box. Having arrived with an early morning local passenger train from Manchester and turned the 'Clan' on the triangle, the crew chat with Jim while awaiting the 'right away' from the signalman before crossing over the junction to run tender-first to Mold Junction. They will return with a Mold Junction - Patricroft goods train and then *Clan MacKenzie* will take out a Manchester-Glasgow express.

*Left*: The conversion of the GWR shed into a diesel multiple unit depot was completed in early 1961 and in June what became Class '108' units under TOPS took over most local trains between Birkenhead and Helsby, Birkenhead and Chester, and Chester and Liverpool Lime Street. All the sets for these services were based at Chester West diesel depot; the depot closed in November 1998. In the foreground is Fairburn 2-6-4T No. 42240 which will take over an incoming Paddington-Birkenhead express for the last leg of its journey. Originally a Scottish Region engine, it was allocated to Corkerhill until transferred to Chester Midland in February 1960 and was there until June 1965.

# CHAPTER 5 - CHESTER AND MOLD JUNCTION

## Chester Northgate station

Northgate was the terminus of the Cheshire Lines Committee line from Manchester Central to Chester via Northwich and was opened in 1875. In March 1890 the Manchester Sheffield & Lincolnshire Railway (which became the Great Central Railway in 1897) opened a line from Hawarden Bridge to meet the CLC line at Chester, thus creating a through route between Chester and Wrexham over the MS&LR line from Shotton.

In 1896 the MS&LR extended its line from Hawarden Bridge to Bidston, and then to Seacombe on the banks of the Mersey in 1898, enabling a through service to there to be introduced from Northgate. Little changed over the next fifty years and the 1923 grouping had minimal effect with the same former Great Central classes continuing to operate passenger services until the early 1950s. In 1956 on each weekday there were eleven trains to Manchester Central, eight to Shotton High Level, two to Buckley Junction and six running through to Wrexham Central.

After the Wrexham and New Brighton services were withdrawn in September 1968 a DMU service to Manchester continued for another year but the station was finally closed in October 1969, when this service was diverted to Chester General.

In 1949 *The Railway Observer* reported that the 'C13' 4-4-2Ts '*had a virtual monopoly of passenger trains between Wrexham (Central) and Chester (Northgate)*' but by 1954 it said '*BR Standard 2-6-2Ts 84000-3 transferred from Plodder Lane ... have largely replaced the G.C. C13 4-4-2Ts on passenger services.*'

Two of Northgate shed's five Robinson 'C13' 4-4-2Ts are in the station; on the left No. 67436 was built in 1905 as GCR No. 359, renumbered by the L&NER in 1924 as 5359 and 7436 in 1946. It was allocated to Northgate from before nationalisation until withdrawn in February 1956. No. 67414, on the right, was built in 1903 as No. 179, renumbered as 5179 in 1924 and 7414 in 1946. It was allocated to Northgate until June 1954 when it moved to Rhosddu from where it was withdrawn a year later.

Parker 'J10/4' 0-6-0 No. 65158 shunting at Chester Northgate on May 14, 1953. It was allocated to Northwich until March 1958 when it moved to Woodford Halse for its last two years in service. No. 65158 had been in service over half a century, having been built by Beyer, Peacock & Co. for the Great Central Railway in 1897 as No. 831. The L&NER renumbered it to 5831 in 1924 and then to 5158 in 1946; it was withdrawn in December 1959.

*R.O. Tuck/Rail Archive Stephenson*

Robinson 'D10' 'Director' 4-4-0 No. 62658 *Prince George* at Chester Northgate station on 14th May 1953. The class was used on the Cheshire Lines Committee in their final years and *Prince George* would be on a working back to Manchester Central. It was allocated to Northwich from October 1948 until withdrawn in August 1955. No. 62658 was built in November 1913 as GCR No. 437 and named *Charles Stuart Wortley* until 1917 when the Director himself became Baron Stuart Wortley and the name of the King's fifth child was substituted. *R.O. Tuck/Rail Archive Stephenson*

One of the so-called 'Improved Directors' built in 1920 as GCR No. 508, 'D11' 4-4-0 No. 62662 *Prince of Wales* departs from Northgate on 6th August 1956. The most important improvement from the ten 'D10's was the use of inside admission piston valves instead of outside admission valves, and a side-window cab was provided. No. 62662 had been transferred to Northwich in May 1956 and was there until mid-1958. The large goods shed built by the Cheshire Lines Committee which was closed in April 1965 is in the background. The sidings and depot on the left were carried over the approach lines into General station on two separate bridges. *J.F. Davies/Rail Archive Stephenson*

BR Standard Class '2' 2-6-2Ts were transferred from Plodder Lane to Wrexham Rhosddu in March 1954 when passenger services between Bolton Great Moor Street and Manchester Exchange were withdrawn and they took over the passenger work from the 'C13' 4-4-2Ts. However, they had all left by mid-1956 to work on the Wirral push-pull services (see chapter 4) and were replaced by the earlier Ivatt LM&SR version. One of the latter, No. 41235, waits in Platform 1 at Northgate on 3rd March 1956 with a Wrexham train. It had been transferred to Rhosddu from Northgate shed in October 1955 and was there until June 1957. The twin pitched roofs in the CLC station were still intact at this date; the one on the left was removed in the late 1950s. Platform 1 was usually used by the trains to Manchester and Platform 2 for those to Wrexham or the Wirral.

The second pitched roof on the eastern side of the station over Platform 2 was demolished in the late 1950s leaving only the one over Platform 1. Three diesel multiple units are together at Northgate in the mid-1960s, with a large number of passengers leaving the arrival in Platform 1. This was one of the later Class '108' units built with a four-character headcode box, these taking over all of the regular passenger services from Northgate from early 1960. The Chester Northgate to Wrexham and to New Brighton services were withdrawn on 9th September 1968 but Northgate station retained an hourly DMU service to Manchester for another year. The station was closed on 6th October 1969, when a new connection had been added at Mickle Trafford, allowing the Manchester service to be diverted to Chester General.

*Kenneth Field/Rail Archive Stephenson*

## Chester Northgate engine shed

Northgate engine shed was built by the Cheshire Lines Committee in 1875 and was re-roofed shortly after nationalisation. It was coded 6D from May 1950 when it came under the 6A Chester District after the redistribution of the Trafford Park district. It closed to steam at the end of 1959 when DMUs took over its passenger work in January 1960.

When the London Midland Region took over responsibility for the shed from the Eastern Region in November 1948 the allocation of eight engines comprised two 'J10' 0-6-0s, four 'C13' 4-4-2Ts and two 'N5' 0-6-2Ts. By the start of 1954 the number on its books had more than doubled to eighteen with five Ivatt 2-6-2Ts joining an increased number of the three Great Central classes. The last of the GCR engines left in May 1958 but the 'O4' 2-8-0s from Northwich continued to work in for another year.

Robinson 'C13' 4-4-2T No. 67400 outside the shed on 13th June 1953. It was allocated to Northgate from March 1947 until November 1955 when it moved to Rhosddu. These engines had been the mainstay of Great Central and then L&NER passenger services between Chester, Wrexham and the Wirral since 1905 but from 1954 began to be displaced by BR Standard and later LM&SR Ivatt 2-6-2Ts.

Gorton's Robinson 2-8-0 No. 63600 at Chester Northgate on 26th September 1954. Rebuilt as an 'O4/7' with a shortened 'O2' boiler in 1942, it carried six different numbers during its 51 years' service beginning in November 1911 as GCR No. 335. It became L&NER No. 5335 in 1924, 3508 in January 1946, 3600 in February 1947, then BR E3600 in January 1948 and finally 63600 in October 1949. The signal box in the background was opened in 1889 to control the junction immediately outside Northgate station after the Great Central Railway Hawarden Bridge line was opened; the GCR route left on the western side of the triangular junction and the Cheshire Lines Committee line to Northwich and Manchester used the eastern side.

GCR 'J10/4' 0-6-0 No. 65140 with another of the class outside Northgate shed on 8th September 1956. It had been transferred there from Northwich in April 1953 but would leave for Wigan Springs Branch at the end of the year. No. 65140 had been built for the Great Central by Beyer, Peacock & Co. Ltd in 1896.
*J.F. Davies/Rail Archive Stephenson*

The ex-Great Central classes at Northgate had all been replaced by LM&SR and BR Standard designs by 1958. Class '2MT' 2-6-0s Nos 78055 and 78038 were there on 2nd June 1957. No. 78055 went new to Northgate in August 1956 and No. 78038 came from Bescot in October 1956 in exchange for an Ivatt Class '2' 2-6-0. When Nos 78055-78059 were allocated there, this was probably the first time Northgate had ever received brand new engines in its entire life! The round topped structure to the left of No. 78055 is the entrance to the air raid shelter. *J.F. Davies/Rail Archive Stephenson*

# 6 – Chester to Denbigh and Denbigh to Rhyl

The Mold Railway Company was authorised in 1847 to build a ten miles long line from a junction with the Chester & Holyhead Railway at Saltney Ferry to Mold. The company ran into financial difficulties, but the line was opened in August 1849 and was worked from the outset by the Chester & Holyhead which took over the company by the end of the year.

The remaining 14¾ miles to Denbigh was built by the Mold & Denbigh Junction Railway and was opened in September 1869. It reached Denbigh using running powers over the Vale of Clwyd Railway from Denbigh Junction, about a mile north of Denbigh.

The Vale of Clwyd Railway, which had been opened in 1858 from Foryd Junction on the Chester to Holyhead Railway to Denbigh, had been absorbed by the London & North Western Railway in 1868. At Denbigh it met the Denbigh, Ruthin & Corwen Railway which had completed its line to Corwen in 1864. Although the Mold & Denbigh Junction Railway remained nominally independent until the 1923 Grouping, the line was always worked by L&NWR. The Vale of Clwyd passenger service between Rhyl and Denbigh ended in September 1955 and that between Chester and Denbigh was withdrawn in April 1962, although freight working continued until 1983 to the Synthite Sidings west of Mold, via the connection from the WM&CQJR at Penyffordd.

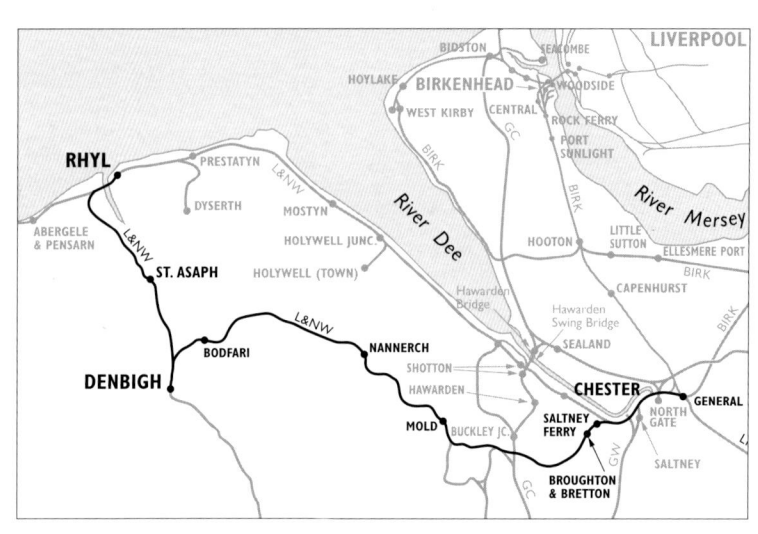

**Saltney Ferry**

With Mold Junction shed in the background, Ivatt Class '2' 2-6-0 No. 46423 pulls out of the island platform at Saltney Ferry with a train to Denbigh, probably in 1956. It was built by British Railways in November 1948 and was at Rhyl from April 1956 until March 1958. The station, which was accessed by steps from the Saltney Ferry Road overbridge, was used only by the Denbigh line trains and was closed in April 1962 when the passenger service was withdrawn.

# CHAPTER 6 - CHESTER TO DENBIGH AND DENBIGH TO RHYL

## Broughton & Bretton

Two views of Llandudno Junction's BR Standard Class '4' 4-6-0 No. 75010 at Broughton & Bretton in around 1960. The station which was only 1½ miles from Saltney Ferry was originally plain Broughton, then Broughton Hall from 1861 until 1908 when it became Broughton & Bretton.

*Above*:
There are no passengers and only a railwayman on the platform as the train from Chester pulls in. The main station building which was designed by Francis Thompson was similar to his stations on the Chester & Holyhead Railway; there was a substantial hipped roof brick-built waiting shelter on the opposite platform which quite possibly was built because the station was close to Hawarden Castle, the family seat of W.E. Gladstone, the Prime Minister on four occasions between 1868 and 1894, and the railway felt it should provide suitable accommodation for his use.

*Below*:
The LM&SR-built signal box worked the level crossing over the A55 Chester to Bangor road. However, the distant arm of the combined Up Home and Distant signal in the centre of the picture was controlled by Mold Junction No. 3 signal box. The black and white building in the right background is the Glynne Arms public house which remains open today as 'The New Glynne Arms'. In the distance on the left are the hangars at Hawarden Airport, part of which was taken over by a wartime shadow factory that built Wellington and Lancaster bombers and after the war produced over 28,000 prefabricated homes. The factory is now owned by Airbus and has manufactured the wings for the A320, A330/A340, A350, and A380 aircraft.

**Mold**

On a wet and dreary day in March 1957 BR Standard Class '2' No. 78056 waits with a train for Denbigh at an almost deserted Mold with just a solitary passenger waiting on the opposite platform. The 2-6-0 was allocated to Chester Northgate from new in August 1956 until April 1959 when it moved to Rhyl.

Also in damp and cold weather, Fairburn 2-6-4T No. 42247 at Mold on a Chester to Denbigh train in the early 1960s. It was built at Derby in October 1946 and was a recent arrival at Chester Midland shed having spent the previous fifteen years in Scotland at Polmadie, Greenock and latterly Corkerhill. It was one of several exchanged for the BR Standard 2-6-4Ts which had worked the line since 1956. No. 42247 was withdrawn in August 1965 from Carnforth.

**Nanerch**

Stanier 2-6-4T No. 42431 with a pair of BR Standard non-corridor suburban coaches departs from Nannerch towards Denbigh in 1959. It was built at Derby in 1936, one of the first batch of the two-cylinder variant of the Stanier 2-6-4Ts and had been at Chester since October 1957 and stayed there until February 1963. The Chester-Denbigh trains had been monopolised by L&NWR Webb 5ft 6in. 0-6-2Ts until the Second World War, after which LM&SR 2-6-4Ts and 2-6-2Ts began to replace them and they were all gone by 1950. The signals at Nannerch were operated from a ground frame on the platform and two other ground frames controlled the goods yard and station crossover; all three frames were unlocked by Annett's key. Note the unusual pattern of running-in board which appears to be no more than an ill-proportioned painted piece of wood.

**Bodfari**

With snow on the hilltop of Moel-y-Parc in the background, Ivatt Class '2' 2-6-2T No. 41233 has steam to spare as it waits to leave Bodfari with a Chester to Denbigh train in March 1955. It had been at Bangor since August 1949 but had moved to Rhyl in the previous month for a five month stay, returning to Bangor three months later. It remained there until closure of the shed in June 1965 and then went into store at Llandudno Junction.

## Denbigh

Denbigh shed contains BR Standard Class '2' 2-6-0 No. 78032 and an Ivatt 2-6-2T in March 1955. It was a sub-shed of Rhyl and although rebuilt in 1948/9 it was closed in September 1955 following the withdrawal of the Denbigh to Rhyl passenger service; the siding to the right of the shed led to a turntable that remained in use until 1962. No. 78032 went new to Rhyl in September 1954 but left for Widnes in May 1956. Rhyl had five of the class in 1954/5 and they replaced the LM&SR Class '2' 4-4-0s on the stopping passenger services from Rhyl to Chester, Bangor and Denbigh.

Ivatt Class '2' 2-6-0 No. 46422 adorned with the 'North Wales Land Cruise' headboard is ready to depart towards Corwen from Denbigh on 16th August 1956, the last year that the 2-6-0s worked the train, after which BR Standard Class '4' 4-6-0s took over following the raising of the route restriction from Dovey Junction to Barmouth and along the coast from 'Yellow' to 'Blue'. This was the London Midland Region 'Land Cruise' which went from Llandudno via Rhyl, Denbigh and Corwen to Barmouth Junction, where it reversed and went to Aberdovey. After a stop of almost two hours it returned to Llandudno through Afon Wen, Caernarvon and Bangor. The passengers can enjoy the delights of the local gas works here rather than the 'most magnificent scenery'! Down the platform, the tour guide with her paperwork is organising the tour participants.

BR Standard Class '2' 2-6-0 No. 78056 at Denbigh on 23rd March 1959. The station had only a single through platform which therefore had to be used in both directions as shown. It was an operating inconvenience because trains could arrive there from three different directions but, despite plans for a separate Down platform in the 1900s, nothing was ever done. This could lead to the situation where a Down train passed the station on the loop line, stopped and then had to reverse into the through platform. The bay platform on the right was used by Rhyl trains.

## St. Asaph

The fireman of Ivatt 2-6-2T No. 41231 prepares to hand over the single line staff to the signalman at St. Asaph, the principal station between Rhyl and Denbigh, in March 1955. In the early 1950s, the three non-motor fitted engines of this class at Rhyl were usually sub-shedded at Denbigh and worked the trains from there to Rhyl until the branch passenger service was withdrawn in September 1955. The line remained open for freight until 1968 and was used by the 'Land Cruise' trains until 1961. The station was built in an exposed location above the town near to the cathedral and the main building still stands today. St. Asaph was granted city status in 2012 as part of the Queen's Diamond Jubilee celebrations and in area and population is the second smallest city in Britain.

# 7 – Chester to Colwyn Bay

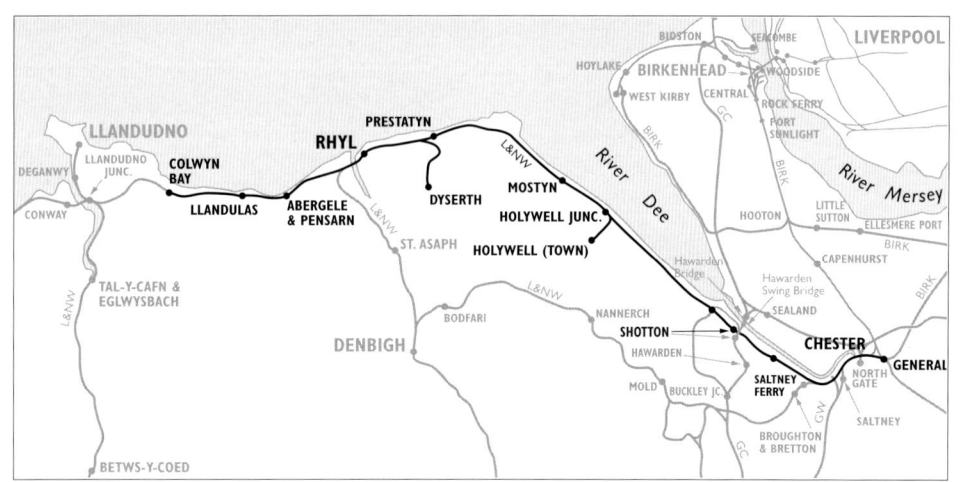

The Chester & Holyhead Railway was authorised in 1844 to build its line which was opened between Chester and Bangor in May 1848 and reached Holyhead in 1850 when the Britannia Bridge over the Menai Straits was completed. After following the estuary of the River Dee from Chester as far as the Point of Ayr, the line continued west along the coast to Colwyn Bay, running almost at the edge of the beach from Foryd onwards. The L&NWR absorbed the Chester & Holyhead in March 1859 after working the line from the outset. Although the anticipated volume of traffic to Ireland did not meet the promoter's expectations, the development of the seaside holiday resorts along the coast brought an increasing amount of traffic which continued to grow up until the 1950s. By the end of the 19th century the L&NWR increased the line's capacity by quadrupling the tracks, apart from the sections from Connah's Quay to Muspratts Sidings west of Flint and from Llandulas to Colwyn Bay; the work was completed in the early 1900s.

**Mostyn**

Two views of BR Standard Class '2' 2-6-2T No. 84003 at Mostyn on 19th August 1963.

*Left:*
A PW man watches as No. 84003 approaches the station from Chester. It was allocated to Rhyl from September 1961 until February 1963 when it moved to Llandudno Junction, staying there until March 1964.

The station when opened in 1848 had two platforms and was double tracked. In the late 19th century/ early 20th century after the line from Saltney Junction to Colwyn Bay was quadrupled, the eastbound platform was converted into an island platform serving the Down Fast and Up Fast lines, and a new platform was built for the eastbound Slow line. The station was closed in February 1966 and within a year the main line was reduced back to double track, the Down Slow in October 1966 and the Up Slow in March 1967. The wagons standing beyond the platform are in the exchange sidings for the industrial line to Mostyn Docks which primarily handled imported sulphur for the Associated Octel works at Amlwch, the traffic lasting until 1988.

CHAPTER 7 - CHESTER TO COLWYN BAY

The English Electric Type '4' diesel-electrics were the mainstay of the North Wales main line passenger services from the mid-1960s until the end of the 1970s. No. D305 approaches Mostyn with a Down express on 24th September 1966. No. D305 was the first of the class built by Robert Stephenson & Hawthorn at Darlington and became No. 40105 under TOPS; it was withdrawn at the end of 1980. In the background is the Mostyn Ironworks which was opened in 1802 to take advantage of the coal produced at Mostyn Colliery. Although the colliery closed in 1884 after flooding, iron production continued using coke brought in from South Yorkshire. The works was extensively rebuilt in the early 20th century and operated until 1965. At the date of this picture it was being demolished by T.W. Ward Limited of Sheffield. *Brian Stephenson*

## Prestatyn

A Down express hauled by 'Coronation' 4-6-2 No. 46242 *City of Glasgow* approaches Prestatyn at milepost 205 on 24th September 1960 in a picture taken from the A548 road-bridge looking east. On the horizon the Down line signals which were controlled by the five-lever Nant Hall box are just visible.

After they were displaced by Type '4' diesels on the West Coast main line, the 'Coronations' were seen more frequently on the North Wales main line. *City of Glasgow* was at Camden from November 1954 until March 1961 when, appropriately, it was transferred to Polmadie for its final years in service. No. 46242 was almost a completely new engine after it was rebuilt following the Harrow & Wealdstone disaster in October 1952. Although the boiler was salvaged the frames were beyond repair and No. 46242 received the front frames and cylinders from No. 46202 *Princess Anne*, after which what was left of that engine was scrapped. This resulted in a curved drop front end platform instead of the open type on all the other de-streamlined 'Coronations'.

BR-built Stanier Class '5' 4-6-0 No. 44712 approaches Prestatyn station with a Saturday extra to the coast in the mid-1960s. Its final shed was Holyhead, from June 1963 until withdrawn in November 1966. The two cars in the station car park are a Vauxhall Victor 'F'-type Estate and an Austin A40. On the right is the original Chester & Holyhead station building, in front of the goods shed.

Edge Hill Class '5' 4-6-0 No. 44772 with a Saturday relief in May 1962. This was the second Prestatyn station, opened in 1897 when the line was quadrupled; the original timber platforms were replaced in the 1950s with concrete platforms. Note the lower line on the running-in board 'FOR PRESTATYN HOLIDAY CAMP'; this had been opened in 1939 as a joint venture between the LM&SR and the Thomas Cook travel company who had planned to open similar camps elsewhere but for the intervention of the Second World War. The camp was sold to Pontins in 1975 and was closed in 1985.

# CHAPTER 7 - CHESTER TO COLWYN BAY

**Dyserth Branch**

The L&NWR opened a short, 2¾ miles long branch from the main line at Prestatyn to Cwm in 1869. It was used only for goods traffic until 1905 when a passenger service to Dyserth, about a mile from Cwm, was started but this only lasted until 1930. It was notable for being the first L&NWR branch to be operated by steam railmotor. Steam power, latterly a Class '5' 4-6-0, was used on the freight trains until the end of 1966 when Chester based Type '2' diesels took over. There was only one train each day, running to the limestone quarry at Dyserth, and this operated until September 1973 when the line was closed.

This series of pictures show BR Sulzer Type '2' diesel-electric No. D5140 working the branch in April 1967. It was built at Darlington in November 1960 and was always on the London Midland Region, starting at Longsight, then in the London area from January 1962 until September 1966, when it moved to the D05 Stoke Division which provided the motive power for Chester and North Wales. It was renumbered to 24140 in 1974 and was withdrawn in January 1976.

No. D5140 waits at the start of the branch with Prestatyn signal box in the background. There was no run-round facility at Dyserth and trains had to be propelled up the 1 in 45 and 1 in 55 gradients. No. D5140 will have to use the loop in the centre of the picture to move to the rear of the train before proceeding towards Dyserth.

No. D5140 propels the empty wagons it has brought in. The line on the left running behind the loading gauge led to the quarry works which was immediately to the north of the town's High Street.

There is something happening beyond No. D5140 which has left the wagons; one man looks on while the one designated as shunter is engaged coupling up the loaded wagons standing on the quarry line.

In the left background is the Vale of Clwyd Farmers' Store. The brake van which accompanied the descending wagons is in the background.

Immediately above the first wagon is the roof of the small wooden station building which was still extant as late as 1979, almost fifty years after passenger services ended.

Man and dog watch on as No. D5140 waits with loaded wagons to take to Prestatyn. The stone-built goods shed had been out of use since general freight ceased in 1951 although coal traffic continued until 1964.

## Rhyl

In July 1950 a push-pull service was introduced running between Rhyl and Llandudno under the title 'The Welsh Dragon', using an Ivatt Class '2' 2-6-2T decorated with a large headboard incorporating a Welsh dragon in red on a green background; a similar board was carried on the rear coach. The train made seven trips each way, Mondays to Fridays only, and was allowed thirty minutes for the 17½ mile journey in the Down direction and thirty-one in the Up direction. For the 1952 season No. 41320 was transferred to Rhyl from Crewe North in July and stayed for eleven weeks. It was the first of the final batch of ten which for some unexplained reason were built at Derby at an increased cost of over £2,000 each when the previous 120 in the class were from Crewe.

Two holidaymakers watch a double-headed Up express arrive at Rhyl. At the front is Stanier 2-6-4T No. 42451 which was at Chester Midland from February 1948 until Autumn 1956 when it was transferred to Newton Heath. Behind is BR Standard Class '5' 4-6-0 No. No. 73020 which went new to Chester Midland in October 1951 together with Nos 73021 and 73022; it was then transferred to Chester West in September 1953 which suggests the date of this picture as early 1952.

North British Locomotive Company-built LM&SR 'Compound' 4-4-0 No. 41157 draws empty coaching stock out of the carriage sheds at Rhyl. It was allocated to Chester Midland shed from 1948 until the end of 1957 when it went to Trafford Park. Rhyl No. 1 signal box on the left was the last box in operation at Rhyl.
*Kenneth Field/Rail Archive Stephenson*

'Jubilee' 4-6-0 No. 45721 *Impregnable* waits with a Down express in the 1950s. It is paired with an 'Old Standard' 3,500 gallon tender with snap-head rivets between 1948 and July 1959, when it reverted to a Stanier 4,000 gallon tender which it kept until withdrawn in 1965. No. 45721 was at Crewe North from January 1955 until November 1959.

CHAPTER 7 - CHESTER TO COLWYN BAY

Patricroft's Stanier Class '5' 4-6-0 No. 45021 arrives at Rhyl with a Down express in summer 1957. It was at the Manchester shed for just three months, from June until September. No. 45021 was the second of the class to be built, emerging from Vulcan Foundry in August 1934, and still has the scalloped steampipes which only the first ten engines had. Note that there were no platforms on the Fast lines, or the through lines as they were commonly known.
*Kenneth Field/Rail Archive Stephenson*

In a picture taken from the Vale Road overbridge in the previous view, 'Royal Scot' No. 46166 *London Rifle Brigade* from Crewe North threads its way over the east end pointwork at Rhyl with a ten-coach Down express, probably on the same day as the picture above. No. 46166 was one of the final batch of twenty built at Derby in 1930, and was rebuilt with a taper boiler in January 1945. In the background to the left of the carriage shed is the impressive signal gantry worked from Rhyl No. 1 signal box.
*Kenneth Field/Rail Archive Stephenson*

BR Caprotti Class '5' 4-6-0 No. 73137 arrives at Rhyl with a Up train. There is nice detail of the BR '1C' 4,725 gallon 9-ton tender with gangway doors and tender cab to protect the crew from the elements. No. 73137 was built at Derby in November 1956 and was at Holyhead until May 1958. In the background are numerous parked coaches – the competition which was killing off the railway's holiday traffic. *Kenneth Field/Rail Archive Stephenson*

Three packed BR Derby lightweight two-car DMUs leave Rhyl on the 'Welsh Dragon' service to Llandudno. The 1957 season began on 17th June using four cars which was increased to six cars at peak times. Note the coach boards bearing the train name – this was very unusual on a Diesel Multiple Unit. The engine shed with a 'Compound' 4-4-0 and an Ivatt 2-6-2T is on the left, the two Down bays are off-centre to the right and on the extreme right is the goods shed, which was accessed from the loop running behind the station. Note the empty coaches standing between the station and the goods yard; the carriage sheds and sidings were frequently over-run with stock at this time. *Kenneth Field/Rail Archive Stephenson*

Two classes which would not have found their way down the North Wales coast in pre-grouping days at Rhyl in 1959. The shed had a number of L&YR engines on its allocation throughout the first decade after nationalisation together with several L&NWR 'Cauliflower' 0-6-0s. It was re-roofed by the LM&SR and coded 7D from 1935, becoming 6K in March 1952 when the former Llandudno Junction Motive Power District was merged into the Chester District. Inside the shed is a BR Standard Class '2' No. 78031 and ex-Midland Railway '2F' 0-6-0 No. 58293, and outside is ex-Lancashire & Yorkshire Railway Class '27' '3F' 0-6-0 No. 52162. No. 52162 was one of the class rebuilt with a Belpaire firebox and was at Rhyl from April 1953 until withdrawn in 1960, whereas No. 58293 did not arrive there until May 1958 and left in December 1959. *Kenneth Field/Rail Archive Stephenson*

'Princess Royal' 4-6-2 No. 46209 *Princess Beatrice* passing under Vale Road Bridge at the east end of Rhyl station with an Up Class 'C' fitted freight in March 1961. It went into store on 12th March, emerging briefly between 16th June and 5th September. It remained in store until 25th January 1962 but returned to service again until finally withdrawn in September 1962. The insulated containers behind No. 46209 would be traffic from Holyhead to Broad Street in London for the Smithfield Meat Market.

Stanier '8F' 2-8-0 No. 48131 hurries through Rhyl station with a Down goods running under Class '8' lamps, although the consist of mostly container wagons suggests it could have been at least partially fitted. If the working timetable showed it to be unfitted freight it was railway practice to run the train unfitted. It was one of the first batch of the class built by the LM&SR during the Second World War, at Crewe in April 1941. No. 48131 has a star below the number on the cab side indicating that it had a balanced wheelset. It was fitted with AWS in October 1960 and was at Birkenhead from November 1962 until July 1963 when it was transferred to Mold Junction. The glazed screen in front of the carriage sidings is visible immediately to the right of the engine.
*Kenneth Field/Rail Archive Stephenson*

'Patriot' 4-6-0 No. 45523 *Bangor* with an Up express, looking towards Colwyn Bay from the footbridge at the east end of Marine Lake at Rhyl. It had been rebuilt with a taper boiler in October 1948 and the AWS was fitted in January 1960; it was allocated to Camden between July 1951 and January 1961. No. 45523 is passing Marine Lake, North Wales' only salt-water lake, which is fed from the nearby estuary. A pleasure park was opened in 1895 and hosts numerous water-based leisure activities as well as a miniature railway, which opened in 1911 and is still operating today; its tracks are just visible in the background.

## Abergele & Pensarn

With signs for Bingo prominent on the seaward side of the line and plenty of activity on the promenade, Class '5' 4-6-0 No. 44760 approaches Abergele & Pensarn station with a Holyhead-Manchester express on 6th August 1963. It was one of the first of the class built by British Railways, new to traffic in February 1948, and had been transferred from Rugby to Llandudno Junction in September 1962. These later Class '5's incorporated a number of modifications introduced by H.G. Ivatt to the original Stanier design including self-cleaning smokeboxes, hopper ashpans and rocking firegrates, all of which were intended to reduce maintenance costs in the post-war era.

On a dreary July day BR Sulzer Type '2' No. D5024 on a relief from Birmingham to Llandudno passes one of the caravan parks on the inland side of the line as it approaches Abergele & Pensarn station on 21st July 1966. It was built at Derby in October 1959 and was allocated to the Eastern Region until March 1961 when it was transferred to Willesden. No. D5024 moved to the Birmingham Division at the end of 1965 and became No. 24024 in February 1974. It was in service until 1975 when it was badly damaged after catching fire and was withdrawn.

After it leaves Rhyl the railway runs almost along the beach, separated by the sea wall and sand dunes. A rake of two three-car BRC&W, later Class '104', DMUs climb west up the hill towards Llandulas past a long line of holiday caravans on Abergele sands; Rhyl station is just visible in the background above the second coach. In September 1957 a new fast diesel service was introduced to Llandudno. The journey from Chester took one hour and was advertised as being the fastest timing ever to operate between those points and even given the name 'The Diesel Rapide'. It left Crewe at 11.15am, running all-stations to Chester, then leaving at 11.55am for Prestatyn, Rhyl, Colwyn Bay, Llandudno Junction and Llandudno.
*Kenneth Field/Rail Archive Stephenson*

## Llandulas

Ken Cook took a series of pictures of the varied traffic passing along the North Wales coast at Llandulas during a day at the lineside on Thursday 5th September 1957.

BR Standard Class '4' 4-6-0 No. 75026 with the 'North Wales Radio Land Cruise' train on its return to Afon Wen. This was the Western Region Cruise train which ran on Tuesdays and Thursdays from Pwllheli through Afon Wen, Portmadoc and Harlech then inland to Corwen and over the former Denbigh, Ruthin & Corwen Railway line to Rhyl, where it reversed and ran back along the North Wales Coast as far as Menai Bridge where it took the branch through Caernarvon to terminate at Afon Wen. No. 75026 had been allocated to Oswestry since the start of 1957.
*K.L. Cook/Rail Archive Stephenson*

The only unnamed 'Britannia' No. 70047 with the Up 'Irish Mail' was one of five of the class, Nos 70045-70049 with 9 ton 4,725 gallon tenders, allocated to Holyhead in 1954 to work the 'Irish Mail' and other expresses on the Holyhead-London route. Four of an earlier batch of the class, Nos 70030-70033, went there from new in late 1952 but were transferred away within two months, deemed unsuitable for the London-Holyhead trains because of the limited, 7 ton coal capacity of their BR1 tenders compared with the 9 tons of the 'Royal Scot's which they replaced. Three of the latter quickly returned to Holyhead in their place. *K.L. Cook/Rail Archive Stephenson*

Mold Junction Stanier Class '5' 4-6-0 No. 44971, coupled to a former coal-weighing tender, with a Down train of ballast empties to Penmaenmawr. No. 44971 was one of the most re-allocated Class '5's moving over thirty times during its twenty-four years and was allocated to North Wales sheds from July 1956 until 1966. The LM&SR-built four coal weighing tenders, two in 1946 and two in 1950, to enable accurate measurement of coal consumption but the weighing equipment was taken out of use in the mid-1950s; No. 44971 was paired with this tender from August 1947 until February 1958. *K.L. Cook/Rail Archive Stephenson*

Stanier 2-6-0 No. 42960, on the Up Slow at the start of the four-track section with a stone train from Penmaenmawr, had been transferred to Mold Junction during the previous week after more than six years at Longsight. There must have been a severe wagon shortage as the hopper wagons were designed for iron ore traffic and may well have been overloaded by the volume of ballast; there are even some standard 16T minerals at the rear of the train also carrying ballast. The 'Moguls' were the first Stanier design to enter service and were a taper boiler version of the Hughes-Fowler 2-6-0s and, although mixed traffic engines, they were mainly used on freight work where their 5ft 6in. diameter driving wheels gave them an advantage over the later Class '5' 4-6-0s, which were more suitable for passenger work. The line of caravans on the other side of the embankment each have a hut for additional storage.

*K.L.Cook/Rail Archive Stephenson*

Two pairs of BR Derby lightweight DMUs pass Llandulas signal box with one of the seven 'Welsh Dragon' services running each day between Rhyl and Llandudno.

*K.L.Cook/Rail Archive Stephenson*

In the final picture from 5th September 1957, another Mold Junction Stanier 2-6-0 No. 42971 passes the site of Llandulas station, which closed in February 1952, with an Up cattle train from Holyhead. The shed had a number of the Moguls on its books from the early 1940s and No. 42971 was there from February 1952 until June 1961. Only about half of the cattle trucks are of the BR type based on the GWR design; most of the remainder are of LM&SR origin with a few L&NER standard ones. In the background is Llandulas Viaduct which was a rebuild of an earlier structure that was washed away in the 19th century. No. 42971 is signalled onto the Up Fast line at the start of the quadruple section; the line west of this point remained double track because it would have been too costly to quadruple the Viaduct and Penmaenrhos Tunnel. *K.L. Cook/Rail Archive Stephenson*

## Llysfaen

With the waves breaking onto the beach in the background, 'Coronation' 4-6-2 No. 46237 *City of Bristol* heads the Up 'Irish Mail' on the double track section at Llysfaen on 7th September 1962. It had been transferred from Carlisle Upperby to Kingmoor in April 1962 and was one of the final survivors of the class withdrawn in September 1964. The Great Orme is in the background, mostly obscured by the engine's exhaust.

## Colwyn Bay

'Jubilee' 4-6-0 No. 45722 *Defence* from Camden departs from Colwyn Bay with an Up express in late 1957. *Defence* had been the subject of extensive testing in an attempt to improve its steaming at the Rugby Test Plant the previous year and the results were applied to eight others in the class. The full sweep of the bay round to Rhos-on-Sea shows up well in the background and the Great Orme is visible above the cab of No. 45722. The hill on the left is Bryn Pydew and the line runs to its left on the way to Llandudno Junction.

Stanier Class '5' 4-6-0 No. 45045 leaves Colwyn Bay with an Up express formed of a motley collection of former LM&SR and GWR stock in 1951. It had been transferred to Holyhead in July 1951 and would stay there until September 1956. Like Compound No. 40926 below it was built at Vulcan Foundry, one of the first thirty of the class, entering service in October 1934. This picture was taken from Colwyn Bay No. 1 signal box, where the line reverted to double track. It was closed in 1968 when the Down Slow line was taken out of use and No. 2 signal box was also closed; a new box was built at the west end of the station. The left-hand span of the station footbridge and the main station buildings were removed in the early 1980s as part of the A55 improvements. In the right background across the bay is the neighbouring resort of Rhos-on-Sea.  *J.D.Mills/Rail Archive Stephenson*

'Compound' 4-4-0s worked most of the North Wales expresses in the first few years after nationalisation until replaced by Stanier 4-6-0s in the early 1950s. No. 40926 from Crewe North departs from Colwyn Bay with a Down express during 1951. It was built by Vulcan Foundry for the LM&SR in May 1927 and was in service for just over thirty years. Note the signals with co-acting arms – the very tall posts allowed them to be sighted from beyond the station footbridge as can be seen in the picture of No. 45045 above.  *J.D.Mills/Rail Archive Stephenson*

CHAPTER 7 - CHESTER TO COLWYN BAY

Crewe North's parallel boiler 'Patriot' Class 4-6-0 No. 45510 produces an impressive smoke display for the cameraman as it leaves Colwyn Bay with a Down express in 1951. It was one of the early members of the class ordered after William Stanier became Chief Mechanical Engineer of the LM&SR in 1932, and although officially classed as rebuilds of former L&NWR 'Claughton' 4-6-0s, in reality little more than the radial bogies were retained. In the background is the headland that prevented the railway from following its coastal alignment and resulted in the boring of Penmaenrhos Tunnel.
*J.D. Mills/Rail Archive Stephenson*

Crewe North 'Jubilee' 4-6-0 No. 45724 *Warspite* leaves Colwyn Bay on the Down Slow with a Euston to Llandudno train in August 1952. It was at Crewe between September 1950 and August 1952 when it was transferred to Carlisle Kingmoor. It had an 'Old Standard' 3,500 gallon tender from 1948 until 1959. The building on the right belonged to the long defunct Chester Engineering Company Ltd and was demolished when the A55 North Wales Expressway was built on the alignment of the railway after the Down lines were removed. The track on the right is the headshunt for the goods yard which was to the south of the station and at a lower level.

*J.D. Mills/Rail Archive Stephenson*

CHAPTER 7 - CHESTER TO COLWYN BAY 143

Two views of 'Coronation' 4-6-2 No. 46235 *City of Birmingham* at Colwyn Bay with the 11.7am departure to Holyhead on 8th June 1960. No. 46235 was selected for preservation in the National Collection and was to be exhibited in its namesake city. After it was taken out of service in September 1964 it was stored at Crewe North until January 1965 and then taken to Nuneaton, remaining there until October, when it went into Crewe Works to be prepared for display and repainted in its final livery of green, lined in orange and black. It went to the Birmingham Museum of Science and Industry in May 1966 and was there until the museum closed in 1997. *City of Birmingham* was subsequently moved to its replacement, the Thinktank, Birmingham Science Museum at Millennium Point, which opened in 2001.

# 8 – Llandudno Junction and Llandudno

After Colwyn Bay the Chester to Holyhead line turns away from the sea and cuts across the Great Orme peninsular to Llandudno Junction on the banks of the Conway estuary. A short distance before Llandudno Junction the Conway Valley line from Blaenau Ffestiniog meets the main line, and immediately to the west of the station the line to Llandudno station curves away from the Holyhead line which crosses the estuary into Conway. This 3 miles 286 yards long branch was built by the St. George's Harbour & Railway Company in 1853 that was taken in 1873 over by the L&NWR, which had operated the line from its opening.

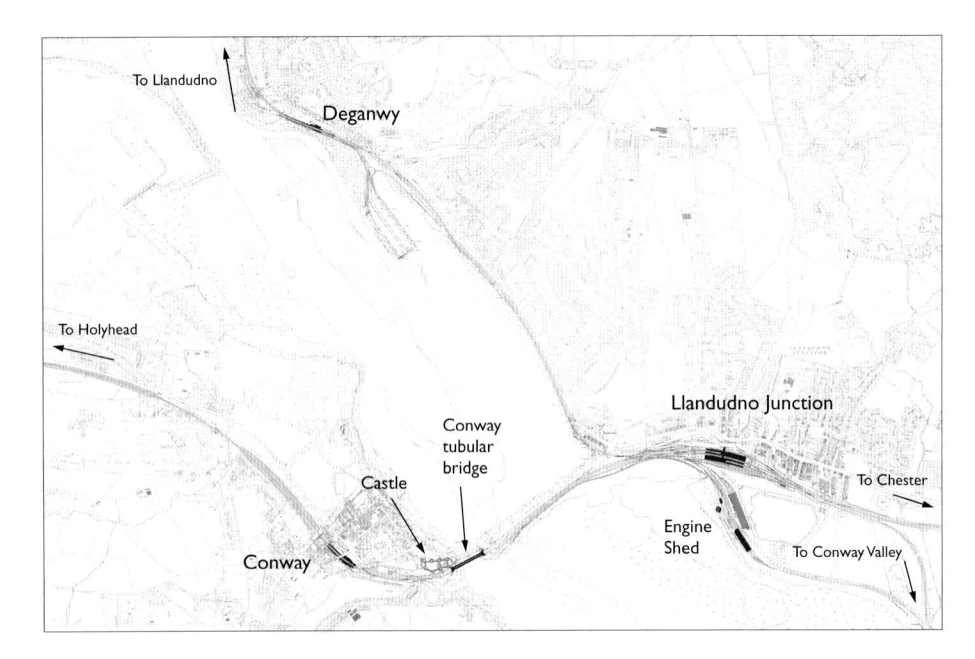

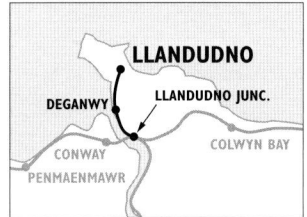

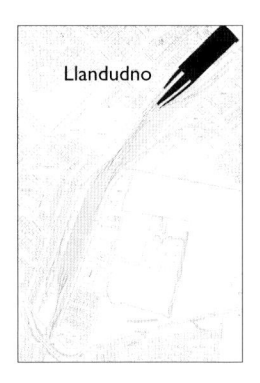

**Llandudno Junction – the east end**

On a busy summer Saturday a Down Relief express from Manchester headed by a very lime-scaled Hughes/Fowler 'Crab' 2-6-0 No. 42715 approaches Llandudno Junction, passing a departing Up express on 4th August 1951. A Conway Valley Branch train from Blaenau Ffestiniog headed by a 2-6-2T is held by the signal in the right distance.

Horwich-built No. 42715 was one of the earliest 'Crabs', entering service in April 1927. It was at Newton Heath from February 1950 until January 1960, its fourth spell at the shed.

BR Standard '9F' 2-10-0 No. 92080 restarts from a signal check with a Down holiday train outside Llandudno Junction. On the right, a Diesel Multiple Unit waits to come off the Conway Valley line. No. 92080 was at Wellingborough between March 1958 and July 1963. The use of the London Midland Region 2-10-0s on summer Saturday holiday trains started in 1957 replacing less suitable types, particularly the '4F' 0-6-0s; the practice lasted until around 1963 as diesel power became more widespread. On Saturdays during the peak holiday periods it was not uncommon for trains to reach Llandudno Junction anything between thirty and ninety minutes late as trains backed up almost back to Chester if there were any untoward incidents.

*Kenneth Field/Rail Archive Stephenson*

'Royal Scot' No. 46162 *Queen's Westminster Rifleman* leaves Llandudno Junction on the Up Fast line with a returning holiday express formed of ER/NER stock. The train is leaving Platform 1 and therefore has probably come from Llandudno, avoiding the conflicting line from Holyhead. This picture was taken after April 1959 when No. 46162 was fitted with AWS and before November 1959 when it was transferred from Camden to Kentish Town. In the background the station is busy with two DMUs in the Conway Valley bays and two trains occupying the Fast through platforms. On the extreme left the glazed weather screen is visible and to its right is the tall 'Llandudno Junction No. 1' signal box which had 101 levers controlling the east end of the station.

*Kenneth Field/Rail Archive Stephenson*

Fowler '4F' 0-6-0 No. 44389 heads east from Llandudno Junction with the shed's breakdown train. It has a tender cab which would be welcomed by the crews when it was used for snowplough duties. No. 44389 was allocated to Llandudno Junction from 1947 until May 1965 when it left for Skipton. The crane is a standard Cowans Sheldon 15 Ton product supplied to the North Staffordshire Railway in 1895. It came to Llandudno Junction shed in 1944 complete with its NSR crane runner wagon. The accompanying tool, packing and mess vehicles are also interesting, the trailing one being converted from a Midland Railway clerestory roofed coach which has been fitted with recessed doors. *Kenneth Field/Rail Archive Stephenson*

Class '5' 4-6-0 No. 44935 on the Down Fast with a train load of empty containers for Holyhead and the Irish meat traffic on 15th August 1962. It would have been a regular sight on the North Wales main line from September 1957, when it was transferred to Llandudno Junction, until it left Mold Junction for Carlisle Kingmoor November 1962.

BR Standard Class '2' 2-6-2T No. 84003 substituting for a DMU on the 'Welsh Dragon' on 15th August 1962. It was transferred to Rhyl from Birkenhead in September 1961 and then moved to Llandudno Junction in February 1963; after a brief spell at Croes Newydd in early 1964 it returned to Llandudno Junction and was withdrawn from there in October 1965. Although the 'Welsh Dragon' had been diesel operated since 1956, the spare stock was still kept in reserve and the headboard stored safely away at the shed.

An Up Class 'D' freight headed by Stanier '8F' 2-8-0 No. 48289 leaving Llandudno Junction on 7th September 1962. No. 48289 which was allocated to Nuneaton from September 1959 until June 1966 was one of the ex-War Department engines bought by British Railways in August 1949; for some reason it assumed the identity 48289 having run in 1940 as LM&SR No. 8299 while the former No. 8289 purchased at the same date became No. 48288. The line on the left is the Down Slow which the Conway Valley Branch to Blaenau Ffestiniog joined a short distance to the east (see Page 148).

Note the diamond crossing and single slip which allowed trains from both the main line and the branch to access all of the lines through the station. The crossover was much more useful to Up trains as it allowed signalled movement from the Up avoider all the way across to the Blaenau line, whereas in the other direction it could only go as far across as the Down Fast. Other movements had to be hand signalled.

Ivatt 2-6-2T No. 41235 brings a freight from Blaenau Ffestiniog off the Conway Valley Branch towards Llandudno Junction on 7th September 1962. When Llandudno Junction station was rebuilt in 1897 the junction was moved half a mile to the east and the original branch formation truncated. No. 41235 was built by British Railways in September 1949 and at this date had only two months left in service. It was one of ten withdrawn in November 1962, the first year in which any of the class were condemned. On the left, a DMU disappears eastwards on the Up Fast line; there were four tracks from here to Colwyn Bay No. 1 signal box.

English Electric Type '4' No. D303 approaches Llandudno Junction with a Down express, probably in 1963. It spent its first few years allocated to Crewe and worked on the Western Division until the late 1960s. After that, it moved around the North West until withdrawal in February 1982 as No. 40103.

*Kenneth Field/Rail Archive Stephenson*

# CHAPTER 8 - LLANDUDNO JUNCTION AND LLANDUDNO

Soon to become a Class '40' under TOPS No. D335 pulls out with a Manchester-bound express in around 1966. It was one of the later batches with split headcode boxes and worked on the LMR Western lines until March 1969 when it went to the Manchester Division. Renumbered as TOPS 40135, it was withdrawn in January 1985 but was reinstated as Departmental use as No. 97406 in May 1985 for use during the remodelling of Crewe station. After its second withdrawal in December 1986, it was purchased by the 'Class 40 Preservation Society' and is currently operational on the national network from its base at the East Lancashire Railway.

## Llandudno Junction station

Most trains on the North Wales Coast mainline, except the Up and Down 'Irish Mail' called at Llandudno Junction, known locally as 'Junction'. The station had two long island platforms and four bay platforms, two at the west end of the Up platform for Llandudno trains and two at the east end of the Down platform for the Conway Valley trains, although about half of the trains ran through between Blaenau Ffestiniog and Llandudno; there was also an avoiding line in each direction outside the platform tracks. The station had been redeveloped at the end of the 19th century because the original station had become congested as traffic increased. An article in the London Midland Region staff magazine, *Roving Reporter*, documented a visit to the station in 1952 and reported that every weekday there were seventy-three through trains calling, twenty-six starting and twenty-six terminating but on summer Saturdays an additional sixty trains had to be handled.

At nationalisation Llandudno Junction had a single L&NWR Webb 2-4-2T which mostly worked light goods traffic on the Llandudno Branch although it was still fitted for 'motor working' of push-pull trains. No. 46604, taking water at the east end of the station, was at the shed from October 1948 until July 1953 when it moved to Bangor. Note the water overflow via the cab floor!

Brand new 'Britannia' No. 70009 *Alfred the Great* departs from Llandudno Junction with an Up express on 13th May 1951. It officially entered service on 4th May allocated to Norwich Thorpe and was observed on the former Great Eastern Railway lines the following week. However, No. 70009 immediately returned to the London Midland Region for a few days until it went to the Southern Region at the end of the month. During this time, it was used for a press run between London and Rugby on 18th May and was probably 'running-in' from Crewe in advance of that when this picture was taken. No. 70009 would end its days on the London Midland Region, at Carlisle Kingmoor from the end of 1963 until withdrawn in January 1967. Note the very unusual Up Fast starter signal with the suspended bracket signals and the miniature signals on the LM&SR-built bracket signal for the Up Slow; the L&NWR signals were replaced in the mid-1950s by modern tubular post signals. The station was well provided with water tanks and three are visible in this picture. The Engine Lie By siding contains two cattle trucks.

*John P. Wilson/Rail Archive Stephenson*

LM&SR 'Compound' 4-4-0 No. 41120 at Llandudno Junction with the 9.48am train from Llandudno on 3rd September 1957. The stock appears to be from the 'Land Cruise' train since the first coach is one of the former 'Coronation Scot' vehicles and the second is a semi-clerestory.

*K.L. Cook/Rail Archive Stephenson*

CHAPTER 8 - LLANDUDNO JUNCTION AND LLANDUDNO

BR Standard Class '4' 4-6-0 No. 75013 arriving at Llandudno Junction with the westbound 'Snowdonian', complete with coach nameboards, in 1959. This was one of the summer holiday services for tourists in North Wales; it ran every weekday from Prestatyn to Llanberis (closed to passengers in the 1930s) taking visitors for Snowdon. If the weather was bad, it made an additional, return trip to Caernarvon during the middle of the day. No. 75013 was allocated to Llandudno Junction between October 1953 and September 1959 when it left for Chester Midland. The 'Snowdonian' was normally the preserve of a 2-6-4T and a tender locomotive was very unusual.
*Kenneth Field/Rail Archive Stephenson*

Two pairs of BR Derby lightweight DMUs with Driving Trailer Composite No. M79652 leading arrive from Llandudno before reversal at the Junction station on a Llandudno to Holyhead working. There are two signal boxes in the background: the large 'Llandudno Junction No. 2' is above the rear vehicle and the 'Llandudno Junction Crossing' box is just visible to the left of the water tower, and behind this is the 'Maelgwyn Hotel'.
*Kenneth Field/Rail Archive Stephenson*

Class '5' 4-6-0 No. 44780 with a Class 'D' freight on the Up Avoiding line on 15th August 1962. It had been transferred to Chester Midland in June 1962 and moved to Llandudno Junction in October, staying there until February 1965. The black and white building in the right background is the Station Hotel which is still in use today, operating as the 'The Old Station Hotel'.

Crewe North 'Jubilee' 4-6-0 No. 45647 *Sturdee* waits in the Down Slow platform on 15th August 1962. No. 45647 became the last 'Jubilee' to visit Llandudno during the summer of 1966 on several weekends working the 09.15 from Leeds on Saturdays and returning with the 13.15 to Manchester Exchange on Mondays. The top of the protective glass screen which ran the length of the building and shielded passengers on Platform 4 from the worst of the elements is visible above the tender. There is a line of tank wagons in front of the carriage shed on the right. These are possibly chlorine tanks for the Octel plant at Amlwch but why they were parked there is not known.

Edge Hill's Class '5' 4-6-0 No. 45249 stands in Platform 3 with a Down express on 6th August 1963; the Llandudno bays are to the left. Note the prototype Stanier tender No. 9000 which was built for 'Princess Royal' No. 6200. It originally had straight side plates similar to the 'Old Standard' 3,500 gallon tenders but was rebuilt with curved top sides in 1935, after which it ran with several Class '5' 4-6-0s ending with No. 45249 in July 1961.

## Llandudno Junction – the west end

'Jubilee' 4-6-0 No. 45556 *Nova Scotia* from Crewe North sets off with the 9.5am Crewe-Holyhead on 4th August 1962. This was a Bank Holiday Saturday and the RCTS carried out a Traffic Survey along the North Wales Coast between Chester and Bangor. This picture and those on the next two pages show some of the trains they recorded on that day. According to the Survey No. 45556 had arrived at Llandudno Junction five minutes late but departed fourteen minutes late; *Nova Scotia* returned with the 4.10pm Holyhead to Birmingham train. There is an interesting mix of fuel oil tanks and banana vans in the yard near the Fyffes depot.

An unusual visitor to North Wales on 4th August 1962 was Polmadie's No. 46222 *Queen Mary* departing from Llandudno Junction with the 9.20am Crewe-Holyhead, which was regularly used as a running-in turn for engines that were ex-works at Crewe. No. 46222 had completed a Heavy General repair on 28th July and would have been working from Crewe North for a few days to ensure everything was in order before returning to Scotland.

*Below*:
Conway Castle is in the background as No. 46222 gets into its stride. It had arrived at Llandudno Junction one minute early but departed two minutes late and dropped another thirteen minutes by Bangor. Note the L&NER Diagram 115 all-door Gresley Corridor Third at the front of the train. This is the corridor side, the other side having doors to each compartment.

With Conway Castle in the background and the line to the quayside, known locally as 'New York', dropping away to the left, BR Caprotti Class '5' No. 73133 brings in the 10.15am Caernarvon-Manchester on 4th August 1962. The services in the Up direction were running much more to time than the Down trains and No. 73133 was recorded by the RCTS Traffic Survey as arriving punctually at Chester.

Caprotti Class '5' 4-6-0 No. 44740 arriving at Llandudno Junction with a Manchester train on 15th August 1962. No. 44740 was allocated to Llandudno Junction shed from new in 1948 until withdrawn in April 1963. It has just passed 'Llandudno Junction No. 2' signal box which had a 154-lever frame to control the operations at the west end of the station.

## Llandudno Junction shed

The first shed built in 1880 on the eastern side of the Conway Valley line was extended to a four-road shed in 1898 after the station was rebuilt in 1897. The original Conway Valley line was severed at the southern end and passed to the Locomotive Department. The LM&SR and later British Railways used it to store engines out of service when not required in the winter months. Towards the end of steam, lines of withdrawn engines congregated there until they could be taken away for scrap. The shed was rebuilt in 1957 with a new roof and a wheel-drop was added. It closed to steam in October 1966. It was coded 7A from 1935 onwards but became 6G in March 1952. The allocation in November 1950 was seven Stanier 2-6-2Ts, ten 'Compound' 4-4-0s, one Ivatt 2-6-2T, two '4F' 0-6-0s, eight Stanier Class '5' 4-6-0s, five of which were Caprotti, one L&NWR 2-4-2, one '3F' 0-6-0T and three L&YR 0-6-0s. The tank engines provided the motive power for the Llandudno and Blaenau Ffestiniog services and were also used as station pilots. By 1954 the pre-grouping classes had gone but otherwise there was little change. There were seven Stanier 2-6-2Ts, two '2P' 4-4-0s, nine 'Compound' 4-4-0s, three Ivatt 2-6-2Ts, two '4F' 0-6-0s, four Stanier Class '5' 4-6-0s, three of which were Caprotti, one '3F' 0-6-0T and five BR Standard Class '4' 4-6-0s. A decade later, dieselisation of the local services had reduced the allocation by a third with five Ivatt and two BR Standard 2-6-2Ts, twelve Stanier Class '5' 4-6-0s, and three '3F' 0-6-0Ts.

A shunter gives the cameraman a hard stare while the fireman balances on the coal on the tender of Lancashire & Yorkshire Railway Aspinall Class '27' 0-6-0 No. 52119 in 1959. The 1891-bullt No. 52119 was allocated to Rhyl from November 1957 until withdrawn in October 1962; by this time, it was used mostly on local trip freight work. On the left is the twin-gabled six-road Carriage Shed with a Stanier 2-6-4T in front, and an '8F' 2-8-0 and a BR Class '4' 4-6-0 are in the shed yard. In the centre is the coaling stage and water tower and to the right is a row of scrap tenders, a mixture of Midland Railway and L&NWR origin, on a headshunt off the turntable line. *Kenneth Field/Rail Archive Stephenson*

The shed viewed from a distance on 5th June 1960 with the carriage shed on the right and the estuary in the background. A variety of types can just be made out including a 'Jubilee', an '8F' 2-8-0, a Stanier 2-6-2T and the inevitable Class '5's, both the Stanier and BR Caprotti varieties. Within three years, the line of stored engines here would stretch away to the left of the picture.

CHAPTER 8 - LLANDUDNO JUNCTION AND LLANDUDNO

Although two of the class had short stays there in the mid-1950s, it was not until November 1959 that Llandudno Junction acquired any more 'Royal Scots' when Nos 46138, 46150 and 46156 arrived. Fourteen different engines were on the shed's books between then and 1964 as diesels displaced them from their former duties. In addition to working the London expresses, one of their regular diagrams was the Manchester 'Club Train', the 7.40am from Llandudno. Both No. 46165 *The Ranger (12th London Regt.)* and No. 46148 *The Manchester Regiment* came from Crewe North in September 1962. The former was there only until June 1963 and the latter stayed until April 1964.

Former Western Region 'Britannia' No. 70017 *Arrow* on shed alongside '8F' 2-8-0 No. 48259 from Mold Junction. *Arrow* has a 6G shedplate but was only allocated to Llandudno Junction for five months between May and September 1963. No. 70017 has the London Midland Region pattern of smoke deflectors with two circular hand-grips rather than the six holes applied by Swindon to most of its other members of the class. The new roof replaced the L&NWR northlight roof in 1957.

## The Llandudno Branch

Stanier Class '5' 4-6-0 No. 44694 from Low Moor shed leaves Llandudno Junction with a holiday train from Bradford to Llandudno and is about to cross the A55 at the level crossing which was a bottleneck for many years until a flyover was built in 1968. The crossing gates were replaced by manned barriers in April 1967 and 'Llandudno Junction Crossing' signal box on the right was closed in June 1969. No. 44694 was built at Horwich in December 1950 and originally had a later pattern boiler with forward top feed but by this date it had been exchanged for an earlier boiler with the top feed immediately in front of the dome. It was withdrawn from Low Moor in September 1967. On the right is 'Llandudno Junction Crossing' signal box and in the left background is the Fyffes banana warehouse; the three sidings in front from left to right were named the Warehouse Siding (with a Banana Van against the stop blocks), Dock Road and Horse Landing. *Kenneth Field/Rail Archive Stephenson*

Hughes-Fowler 2-6-0 No. 42856 approaches Llandudno Junction with an Up holiday train from Llandudno in the summer of 1959. It is signalled into Platform 1 so avoiding the main line from Holyhead. No. 42856 was built as No. 13156 at Crewe in March 1930, was renumbered as 2856 in June 1934 and was allocated to Longsight until 1946. In November 1958 it was transferred from Crewe South to Birkenhead, remaining there until July 1961.

*Kenneth Field/Rail Archive Stephenson*

A Metropolitan-Cammell DMU, with Motor Composite No. M 50324 leading, approaches Llandudno Junction on an excursion returning from Llandudno to Birmingham in 1959. These units became Class '101' under TOPS. DMUs began working excursions from the Midlands to North Wales in 1956; nowadays it may seem an awfully long way to travel in vehicles more suitable for short-distance work, but in 1959 these were the height of luxury and unlike a road coach there was access to a toilet!
*Kenneth Field/Rail Archive Stephenson*

The traffic waits for 'Princess Royal' 4-6-2 No. 46206 *Princess Marie Louise* to back over the A55 level crossing towards Llandudno to pick up the 12.20pm Llandudno to Euston on 4th August 1962. It was described in that day's RCTS Traffic Survey *'as black as the ace of spades'*. Llandudno Junction Crossing signal box which controlled the crossing was an all-timber LM&SR Type '11C' box with ten levers that had replaced a L&NWR cabin in 1950.

## Deganwy

The man on the left is studying the poster board which is advertising the North Wales Land Cruise trains while he waits at the level crossing for Newton Heath's Hughes-Fowler 2-6-0 No. 42705 with an excursion to Llandudno at Deganwy in 1956. Deganwy was about halfway along the branch with a signal box at either end and the main station buildings on the Up side.

Stanier Class '5' No. 44807 from Monument Lane shed in Birmingham arrives at Deganwy with a train for Llandudno in 1959. It was one of the class built at Derby during the Second World War which incorporated a number of minor changes from the pre-war engines, including additional frame stays to combat the problems with cracked frames that had begun to emerge by this date. In the distance Deganwy Quay is immediately above the yachts moored on the Conway estuary.
*Kenneth Field/Rail Archive Stephenson*

Watched by Signal & Telegraph staff, locals and holidaymakers who are waiting to cross over the railway rather than using the footbridge from where the picture was taken, BR Class '5' 4-6-0 No. 73043 departs from Deganwy with a train for Llandudno. The pedestrians will have to wait because another train is signalled from Llandudno. This overhead view shows good detail of the engine and tender with the tender cab and rubber draught excluder providing a high level of comfort for the crew. Deganwy Castle Hotel on the right closed in 2010 and the site has been partially redeveloped for residential use. Its main claim to fame was when it was bought in 1959 by the musician Jess Yates, a local Llandudno man, whose daughter Paula Yates became more famous than him in the late 20th century. *Kenneth Field/Rail Archive Stephenson*

CHAPTER 8 - LLANDUDNO JUNCTION AND LLANDUDNO

Caprotti Class '5' No. 73137 leaves Deganwy on the 2.0pm Llandudno-Manchester. It was allocated to Patricroft from June 1964 until withdrawn in June 1967. Thirty of the BR Standard Class '5' 4-6-0s with Caprotti valve gear were built at Derby in 1956/7 using the final version of the gear which had been incorporated in the last two LM&SR Class '5' 4-6-0s, Nos 44686 and 44687. This later version was markedly better than the earlier application of the gear on Nos 44738-44757.

Patricroft Caprotti Class '5' No. 73127 returning tender-first from Llandudno with Empty Coaching Stock on 5th June 1960. On the right are the open-air swimming baths (the Deganwy West Shore Bathing Pool) which opened in the inter-war years and remained in use until the early 1960s, when they were closed and demolished. Beyond is Maesdu golf course and in the background is the Great Orme. Note the sand which has blown onto the track.

## Llandudno

Caprotti Class '5' 4-6-0 No. 44738 at Llandudno on 13th May 1951. Five of these, Nos 44738-44742, were allocated from new in 1948 to Llandudno Junction; the first three were there until 1963, the other two leaving in 1953. One of their regular duties was on the 'Club' residential expresses, each day one to Manchester Exchange and one to Liverpool Lime Street. These dated back to pre-Grouping days and conveyed businessmen in comfort from their homes on the North Wales Coast into the city for a day's business and returned them home in the early evening.

Llandudno had extensive carriage sidings immediately outside the station, ten double-ended at Cae Mawr on the Down side and nine single-ended at Cae Bach on the Up side, to accommodate the stock off the summer excursion trains. However, it did not have an engine shed, although there was a turntable.

*John P. Wilson/Rail Archive Stephenson*

One of the two 'Jubilee' Class rebuilt with a taper boiler in 1942, No. 45735 *Comet* is ready to depart from Llandudno with a London express in 1961. The rebuilding was deemed a success and led to all seventy 'Royal Scot' 4-6-0s and eighteen 'Patriot' 4-6-0s following suit using the same Type 2A boiler over the following decade or so. *Comet* had been transferred to Willesden from Edge Hill in January 1961 and it worked out its final year from Annesley over the former Great Central line until withdrawal in October 1964. The Metro-Cammell diesel multiple unit alongside has 'Excursion' in its destination panel. Llandudno station was rebuilt in 1892 to cater for the growing volume of traffic and had five platform faces below a three-span overall roof. Two of the platforms were taken out of use in 1978 and the overall roof cut back; the remainder was extensively modernised in 2015 as part of a new Transport Interchange. The goods yard was behind the wall on the right where the tops of a van and several mineral wagons are just visible and the goods shed was attached to the side of the trainshed.

# 9 – The Conway Valley line to Blaenau Ffestiniog

The twenty-seven miles long line down the Conway Valley from Llandudno Junction to Blaenau Ffestiniog was built by the London & North Western Railway and opened in three stages, to Llanrwst in 1863, Betws-y-Coed in 1867 and finally reached Blaenau Ffestiniog in 1879, after a 2 miles 206 yards long tunnel was built through the solid rock of Moel Dyrnogydd. The bore was almost 800 feet above sea level and the tunnel was the eighth longest in Britain at that date.

At its peak immediately before the Second World War, there were eleven passenger trains each way on weekdays, several of which worked through to Llandudno. In the early 1950s the timetable had nine passenger trains and one daily freight. Diesel multiple units were introduced in March 1956, the first in Wales, and were very successful in attracting more passengers to the line, producing a thirty-nine percent increase within the first year. Although the passenger service was proposed for withdrawal in 1964, it survived and is still in operation today.

In 1957 Liverpool Corporation obtained authorisation to build a dam and reservoir in the Tryweryn valley which meant flooding a section of the GWR Bala to Blaenau Ffestiniog Branch which resulted in its closure in 1960, except for the section south to Trawsfynydd. As part of the arrangement, Liverpool Corporation funded the construction of a connection between the Western Region Blaenau Ffestiniog Central station and the London Midland Region station. This was opened in April 1964 to allow for the transportation of nuclear waste from Trawsfynydd to Sellafield; it was mothballed after the power station was de-fuelled and the last train ran in 1997.

**Tal-y-Cafn & Eglwysbach**

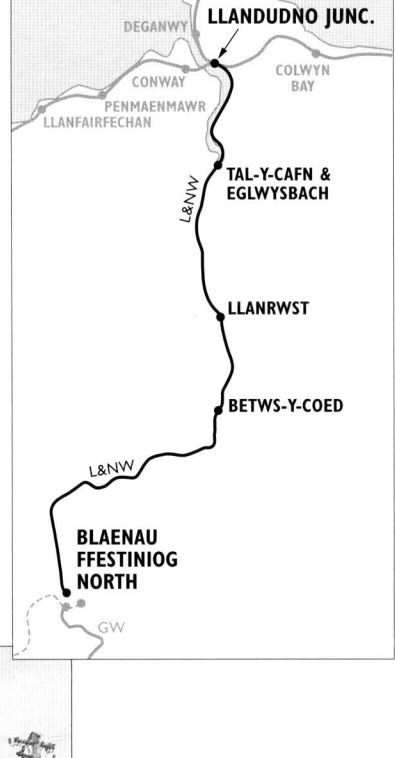

Derby 'Lightweight' DMU Driving Trailer Composite No. M 79683 at the front of a well-packed four-car train at Tal-y-Cafn & Eglwysbach on 30th August 1958. This was the first passing point on the branch and was the nearest station to Bodnant Gardens. Note the low height of the platforms which meant that portable wooden steps had to be provided on each platform for passengers to use when leaving or joining the train.

## Llanrwst & Trefriw

A pair of BR Derby 'lightweight' DMUs wait to leave Llanrwst & Trefriw on a Llandudno to Blaenau Ffestiniog North service after a northbound train has departed in 1959. The first station at Llanrwst was the original terminus of the line from Llandudno Junction and was replaced when the line was extended to Betws-y-Coed. It was provided with a four-road goods yard which handled a large amount of agricultural traffic until the 1960s. The station is now called North Llanrwst after another station more central to the town was opened in 1989. *Kenneth Field/Rail Archive Stephenson*

## Betws-y-Coed

Stanier Class '3P' 2-6-2T No. 40130 leaves Betws-y-Coed with a four-coach train for Blaenau Ffestiniog in 1952, crossing a Llandudno-bound train visible below the footbridge in the background. It was transferred to Llandudno Junction in January 1948 when the shed was coded 7A but now has a 6G shedplate which was the code from March 1952; it was withdrawn from Llandudno Junction in October 1961. The Stanier engines today have a poor reputation but they had been used successfully on the branch passenger service since 1937 when four of them were allocated to Llandudno Junction and they had a virtual monopoly until the early 1950s when Ivatt Class '2' 2-6-2Ts arrived. *J.D. Mills/Rail Archive Stephenson*

CHAPTER 9 - THE CONWAY VALLEY LINE TO BLAENAU FFESTINIOG 167

Brand new Derby 'Lightweight' DMU with Driving Trailer Composite No. M79677 leading arrives at Betws-y-Coed on a Llandudno to Blaenau Ffestiniog North service on 6th June 1956. The Down platform had been extended in 1898 and was almost twice as long as the Up platform. The L&NWR Type '4' No. 1 signal box was at the entrance to the goods yard and on the left is the water tank in what was the former engine shed yard; the shed itself was demolished before the Second World War.
*John Head/Rail Archive Stephenson*

A BR Derby 'Lightweight' DMU approaches Betws-y-Coed on a Blaenau Ffestiniog North to Llandudno service, probably in 1957. The small No. 2 signal box was only 10ft by 8ft and housed an 18-lever frame of which seven were spare. Note that the tall post nearby has signals for both directions of running.
*Kenneth Field/Rail Archive Stephenson*

Stanier Class '3P' 2-6-2T No. 40133 has just arrived at Betws-y-Coed as passengers surge to the footbridge on what was possibly an evening excursion in the late 1950s from Llandudno to visit the Swallow Falls, two miles away on the local bus. It was one of more than half a dozen of the class allocated to Llandudno Junction in the 1950s and was there from May 1948 until withdrawal in October 1961. Betws-y-Coed station was built on a fairly lavish scale with visitors in mind and had a large two-storey station building on the Up side with a large refreshment room occupying much of the ground floor; the upper floor was accommodation for the Station Master and his family. There were extensive goods facilities with a large goods shed, cattle dock and slate wharf.

*Kenneth Field/Rail Archive Stephenson*

# CHAPTER 9 - THE CONWAY VALLEY LINE TO BLAENAU FFESTINIOG

BR Derby lightweight DMU No. M79105 leaves Betws-y-Coed on a Llandudno to Blaenau Ffestiniog North service while another unit going north to Llandudno waits in the station in 1957. There is a Camping Coach alongside the disused slate quay, which was used for end loading only, and the track to the goods shed (now the home of Conway Valley Railway Museum) runs to the right of the platform fence. The size of the station building is apparent in this view.
*Kenneth Field/Rail Archive Stephenson*

## Blaenau Ffestiniog North

Derby 'Lightweight' DMU No. M79126 already has the signal as the guard waits for departure time at Blaenau Ffestiniog on 18th August 1958. The station was at high altitude which meant that wet and dismal conditions with low cloud and rain endured for much of the year and this was exacerbated by the slate waste tips that dominate the scene. One of the raised tranship platforms for the narrow gauge Festiniog Railway line is on the right. The station building dated from around 1957, replacing a 'temporary' wooden hut which had been in use since 1951 after the original station building was demolished. It was renamed Blaenau Ffestiniog North at nationalisation to distinguish it from the former GWR station which became Blaenau Ffestiniog Central.

Ivatt Class '2MT' 2-6-2T No. 41235 waits to follow the DMU from Blaenau Ffestiniog North with the branch goods to Llandudno Junction during 1959. No. 41235 was at Llandudno Junction from September 1957, joining Nos 41236-41238 there, until withdrawn in November 1962. The Ivatt engines worked the daily branch freight from the early 1950s until the mid-1960s, replacing L&NWR 'Cauliflower' 0-6-0s which had been used for many years and which had also worked the passenger trains until the late 1930s. To the left of the water tower in the distance had been a four-road combined engine and carriage shed which was demolished in the 1930s. The platform was extended in 1963 by about 120ft, built up to the level of the timber part of the signal box (see page 171), and a similar amount was removed at the other end as part of the connecting link to Blaenau Ffestiniog Central station.

BR Class '2' 2-6-2T No. 84020 at Blaenau Ffestiniog with a 13T 'Shock' wagon for carrying slate with the inscription 'Empty to Blaenau Ffestiniog North LNW' in 1962. No. 84020 had been transferred to Llandudno Junction in September 1961 from Exmouth Junction when the ten Darlington-built BR engines were transferred to the London Midland Region in exchange for the final ten Ivatt 2-6-2Ts; it was withdrawn from Llandudno Junction in October 1964.
*Kenneth Field/Rail Archive Stephenson*

A DMU waits to leave Blaenau Ffestiniog North with the 7.50pm train to Llandudno on 26th July 1963. The Derby 'Lightweight' units had all been transferred away by this date and replaced by BRC&W sets, later Class '104' under TOPS. The new extension to the platform shows clearly to the left of the signal box around the base of which the longer platform was built. The 14ft by 9ft box was constructed over an exposed L&NWR 18-lever tappet frame in the late 1930s after the original signal box was demolished. The former railway owned North Western Hotel is in the centre background and the connecting link to Blaenau Ffestiniog Central, opened in November 1963, ran under the newly built bridge in front of it.
*Brian Stephenson*

# 10 – Llandudno Junction to Bangor

Immediately after leaving Llandudno Junction the North Wales main line crossed the River Conway through the Conway Tubular Bridge. From Conway it followed the coast almost as far as Bangor and four sea walls had to be constructed, the most difficult engineering work being required between Penmaenmawr and Llanfairfrechan where the line runs on a terrace for over a mile. A 200 yard long tunnel also had to be built there with avalanche shelters at either end to protect against falling rocks. The line turned away from the coast after Aber and reached Bangor through another tunnel, 913 yards long, under the Bangor Mountain.

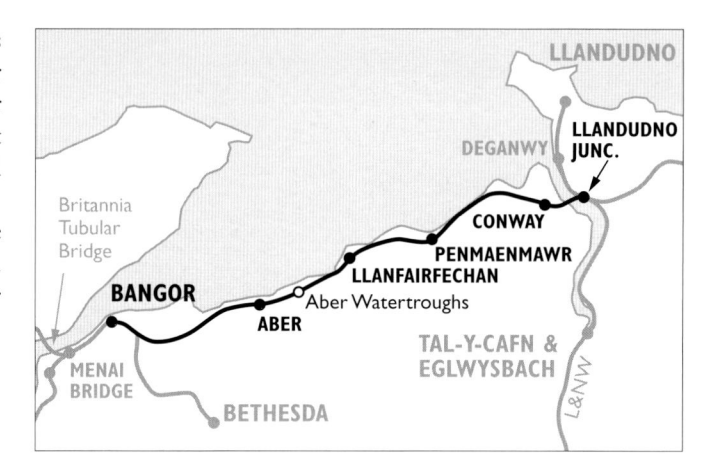

**Conway**

The man on the bowling green does not look up from his game as 'Britannia' 4-6-2 No. 70054 *Dornoch Firth* bursts out of the Conway Tubular Bridge and passes Conway Castle with a Down express. No. 70054 had moved to the London Midland Region in September 1962 from Holbeck where it had been allocated since October 1958. Robert Stephenson's 149 yards long twin-tube bridge over the River Conway was completed in 1848 and had portals designed to complement the castle. The way in which the Chester & Holyhead line was allowed to run through the historic town and castle shows how important the railway was considered when it was built. The castle itself was built for King Edward I in the 13th century and it was completed along with the town walls in only four years, between 1283 and 1287. Each 425 ft long tube was effectively a rectangular 'tunnel' each weighing over 1,000 tons, and they were prefabricated on shore before being floated into place on pontoons and then raised by hydraulic rams over several days. The tubes were fixed to the pier at the Conway end but at the Chester side they rested on cast iron rollers which allowed them to move by around twelve inches. Unlike Stephenson's bridge over the Menai Straits there were no minimum height restrictions and hence only small boats could pass beneath with only 46 feet clearance even at low tide. The bridge was described at the time of its construction as '*one of the greatest scientific achievements of the age*'. In the right distance across the river are the sidings at Conway Quay, which were used for storage of stock and contain a single coach and a few wagons.

*Kenneth Field/Rail Archive Stephenson*

CHAPTER 10 - LLANDUDNO JUNCTION TO BANGOR

Stanier 2-6-4T No. 42478 comes round the curve after passing the castle and approaches Conway station with the 4.22pm Llandudno Junction to Bangor train on 6th September 1957. It had been transferred from Longsight to Bangor in June 1957 but returned to Manchester at Patricroft in September 1958. Conway had a small goods yard on the Up side with sidings serving the town's Corporation Gas Works and the Conway stone quarries, but there is little sign of activity on this day.

*K.L. Cook/Rail Archive Stephenson*

In the second of two pictures taken from the signal box, Stanier '8F' 2-8-0 No. 48188 approaches Conway station with a Down Empty Coaching Stock train also on 6th September 1957. It was built by the LM&SR in April 1942 and was at Warrington Dallam from January 1952 until April 1958.

*K.L. Cook/Rail Archive Stephenson*

BR Caprotti Class '5' 4-6-0 No. 73135 sets off from Conway with the 12.22pm Holyhead to Llandudno Junction stopping train on 6th September 1957. No. 73135 was built at Derby in October 1956 and along with Nos 73136-73139 went new to Holyhead; it remained there until May 1958. The six-plank open wagon on the left is parked in the siding used by the local Signal & Telegraph Department. This picture was taken from Conway Station signal box. It had a bell to warn the station staff that a Down local train had left 'Junction' and to be ready for it. *K.L. Cook/Rail Archive Stephenson*

On the same day, a BR Derby 'Lightweight' DMU leaves Conway on the 3.15pm Bangor to Llandudno Junction service. The set left Llandudno Junction the following month, going to Carlisle Upperby. It has passed through the arched opening cut through the town walls, which were 1,400 yards long and up to 12ft thick and had twenty-one semi-circular towers.

*K.L. Cook/Rail Archive Stephenson*

# CHAPTER 10 - LLANDUDNO JUNCTION TO BANGOR

Stanier 2-6-0 No. 42971 passes through Conway station with an Up Class 'E' freight in 1957. It was built in January 1934 as LM&SR No. 13271 and was renumbered as 2971 in December 1935. No. 42971 was allocated to Mold Junction from February 1952 until June 1961 when it was transferred to Chester Midland. Conway station was within the town walls and had a regular stopping train service until closure in February 1966, shortly after which the station buildings were demolished.

*Kenneth Field/Rail Archive Stephenson*

The 'Snowdonian' tourist train, which ran Saturdays Excepted in the summer season from Rhyl to Llanberis and back, is returning headed by bunker-first Stanier 2-6-4T No. 42487 on 7th September 1962. No. 42487 was allocated to Bangor from June 1959 until withdrawn in September 1963. The station buildings were constructed in a mock-Tudor style in keeping with the surrounding area. After much lobbying by the local politicians, the station was re-opened, with much simpler buildings, in June 1987 as 'Conwy' in an attempt to encourage tourism to the town while the A55 Conwy Tunnel was under construction.

Longsight's Hughes-Fowler 'Crab' 2-6-0 No. 42931 has just passed Conway station with a Down holiday train, probably originating from Stockport or Manchester, in 1957. After leaving the station, the line passes through the 74-yards long Conway Tunnel running under the 13th century town walls. No. 42931 was built at Crewe in June 1931 as No. 13231 and was at Willesden for fifteen years until transferred to Longsight in May 1957.

*Kenneth Field/Rail Archive Stephenson*

A BR Derby lightweight DMU forms the 4.30pm Llandudno Junction to Bangor service approaching Penmaenbach Tunnel from Conway on 26th July 1963. The old A55 road is in the background on the right and above are the scars of the former stone workings on Conway Mountain leading to the sidings at Conway Morfa.
*Kenneth Field/Rail Archive Stephenson*

## Penmaenmawr

WD 'Austerity' 2-8-0 No. 90187 shows how near the line was to the coast at Penmaenmawr as it heads a Menai Bridge-Mold Junction freight away from there in 1958. In 1952 a number of these 2-8-0s were transferred from the Eastern Region at Colwick and Staveley when Mold Junction lost most of its Stanier '8F' 2-8-0s. No. 90187 was one of these, arriving at Mold Junction from Colwick in May 1952; it was there until March 1961 when it moved to Carnforth. In the distance the counter-balance inclines used to bring down the granite from the quarry on Penmaenmawr mountain are visible and on the right is the stone loading facility.

With the coast on the left, 'Britannia' No. 70047 heads the Down 'Irish Mail' through Penmaenmawr on 6th August 1955. This was the only 'Britannia' to remain unnamed although eight groups of names had been suggested in the mid-1950s for Nos 70045-70049 which all went from new to Holyhead in the summer of 1954; the five were transferred away at the end of 1959. The signal box on the right was a replacement for the L&NWR box following the collision on 27th August 1950 between 'Royal Scot' No. 46119 *Lancashire Fusilier* on the Up 'Irish Mail' and a Light Engine, Hughes-Fowler 2-6-0 No. 42885.

'Royal Scot' No. 46138 *The London Irish Rifleman* approaches Penmaenmawr with an Up express from Holyhead, probably in 1960. When built in 1927 it was named *Fury* but this was replaced by the regimental name after *Fury* was transferred to the ill-fated LM&SR high pressure locomotive. No. 46138 was fitted with AWS in May 1959 and had been transferred from Crewe North to Llandudno Junction in November 1959. On the right is a very early signal box, the box featuring in the 1950 accident had been demolished and its base is still visible on the left. In the background, running above the railway is the stone loading facility.

*Kenneth Field/Rail Archive Stephenson*

# CHAPTER 10 - LLANDUDNO JUNCTION TO BANGOR

Fowler '4F' 0-6-0 No. 44525 enters Penmaenmawr station with an Up slow comprising five BR Mark 1 coaches in 1959. It was at Llandudno Junction between November 1954 and December 1964 before ending its days as a Crewe Works shunter until withdrawal in October 1966. In the background is Penmaenmawr which originally rose to a height of around 1,500 feet but was reduced by almost 500 feet due to large scale quarrying of its granite formation from the 1830s onwards. *Kenneth Field/Rail Archive Stephenson*

*Below:* With the Great Orme in the background, a new Derby twin power car DMU, later Class '108', has just arrived at Penmaenmawr on a service to Caernarvon. Several two-car sets were delivered to Llandudno Junction in early 1959 replacing the Derby 'Lightweights'; the batches built from 1960 were fitted with 4-character headcode boxes unlike the earlier examples. Note in the background a WD 2-8-0 with a train of granite from the loading facility at Penmaenmawr, the stone having been conveyed there down the hill and under the A55 road. There was a light railway from the quarry that also crossed the main line on the Down side of the station to exchange stone in the sidings.
*Kenneth Field/Rail Archive Stephenson*

## Llanfairfechan

Derby 'Lightweight' DMU with Motor Brake Second No. M79173 leading waits at Llanfairfechan on the 11.35am Llandudno Junction-Pwllheli on 22nd August 1956. The station was opened in 1860 by the L&NWR and is still open today. The original buildings on the right were demolished in 1987 to make way for the A55 'North Wales Expressway'.

## Aber

With the headland at Penmaenmawr and Penmaenmawr quarry in the background, Stanier 2-6-0 No. 42960 had over-filled its tender tank when it took on water at Aber troughs as it approaches Aber station with a Down Empty Coaching Stock train on 3rd September 1957. The well-travelled 'Mogul' moved sheds no less than twenty-six times during its thirty-two years in service; it was at Mold Junction from August 1957 until April 1960 and ended its days at Heaton Mersey in January 1966. The water troughs at Aber were not the first in the world as sometimes written – those were installed by the L&NWR in 1860 at Mochdre & Pabo, east of Llandudno Junction, but were moved to Aber in 1871 apparently because repositioning them enabled a water stop at Bodorgan on the Isle of Anglesey to be eliminated.

*K.L. Cook/Rail Archive Stephenson*

BR Caprotti Class '5' 4-6-0 No. 73140 in Aber station with the 12.22pm Holyhead to Llandudno stopping train on 3rd September 1957. Although it only entered service in December 1956, No. 73140 is in dreadful external condition. It spent a few weeks at Leicester Midland and was then at Holyhead from January 1957 until May 1958, when it went back to Leicester. Local services on the North Wales coast were under threat well before the Beeching cuts and Aber station lost its passenger facilities in September 1960, and was closed completely in May 1964. The station building was one of Francis Thompson's smaller plain designs for the Chester & Holyhead Railway with a shallow pitched roof and tall chimney stacks.

*K.L. Cook/Rail Archive Stephenson*

Ivatt Class '2' 2-6-0 No. 46433 waits at Aber with a Down local service in the mid-1950s. The 2-6-0s were usually only found on the North Wales coast during the summer timetable with two or three going to Rhyl or Llandudno Junction for a few months in most years from 1951 to 1956, with one of their regular duties working the 'North Wales Land Cruise' trains. The 1956 contingent stayed longer, and No. 46433 was at Rhyl from May 1956 until June 1958. Note the low station platforms dating from Chester & Holyhead Railway days and the 'hawkeye' aluminium running-in board in its custom frame provided by the LM&SR to their standard pattern; these were originally finished with reflective yellow paint. The station served the parish of Abergwyngregyn but the L&NWR, always with a mind to economy, shortened it to Aber.

**Bangor**

'Jubilee' 4-6-0 No. 45666 *Cornwallis* on Bridge 152, the Cegin Viaduct at Llandegai, after it emerges from Bangor Tunnel east of Bangor station with an Up slow. Bethesda Junction signal box, visible through the foliage, controlled access to the Bethesda Branch which diverged off to the left, between the tunnel mouth and signal box. No. 45666 was the second 'Jubilee' to be built with a larger 31 sq.ft grate and sloping throatplate 21-element superheater boiler following a long series of tests and experiments in 1934 and 1935 to improve the steaming of the class. This picture was probably taken in 1951 while *Cornwallis* was allocated to Crewe North, from October 1949 until February 1953 when it left for Carlisle Upperby. It was the last of fifty of the class built with a smaller 3,500 gallon Stanier tender. It returned to Crewe North for two further periods in 1959 and 1961 but was withdrawn from Warrington Dallam in April 1965.

*J. D. Mills/Rail Archive Stephenson*

# CHAPTER 10 - LLANDUDNO JUNCTION TO BANGOR

The east end of Bangor station looking down from Bangor Mountain with Bangor No. 1 signal box in the foreground. Further away the engine shed is on the left and in the centre is the two-storey station building with its white brickwork built by the Chester & Holyhead Railway; the impressive station entrance with ornamental iron gates was on the Holyhead Road to the right. A Caprotti Class '5' 4-6-0 waits in the Up platform with a three coach local train and a Derby 'Lightweight' DMU stands in the short bay platform off the Down passenger loop built specifically for the Bethesda Branch trains when the station was modernised between 1924 and 1927. Bangor No. 1 signal box which had a 63-lever frame also dates from this time when it replaced an older box which was on the Down platform. The Down loops are occupied by empty coaching stock and there is an excellent view of the top of the L&NWR water tank and its walkways – ideal for modellers. In the distance are the portals of Belmont Tunnel with Bangor No. 2 signal box to the right. The station occupied a cramped site between two hills with a 913 yard tunnel at the east end and the 615 yard Belmont Tunnel at the west end. The latter was originally 726 yards and was shortened during the modernisation work.

In July 1948 Bangor had the largest number of ex-L&NWR engines in North Wales but these quickly dispersed in the next few years, mostly for scrap. 0-6-2T 'Coal Tank' No. 58903 at Bangor on 14th December 1951 was built in 1885 and was the last of these tanks to remain there. It was used for shunting at Bangor but spent the last two months in service at Monument Lane working as Birmingham New Street station pilot before it was withdrawn in June 1954. The former shedmaster at Bangor, J. M. Dunn, was instrumental in securing one of the 'Coal Tanks' for preservation; BR No. 58926 is now owned by the National Trust and is now based on the Keighley & Worth Valley Railway under the care of the Bahamas Locomotive Society.

*R.O. Tuck/Rail Archive Stephenson*

'Britannia' No. 70045, named *Lord Rowallan* in July 1957, at Bangor in the mid-1950s with a Down 'Ordinary Passenger' train. It was one of five of the class allocated to Holyhead from new in 1954 until the end of 1959 when they were replaced by English Electric Type '4' diesels. The distinctive towers in the background contain the electric luggage lifts, built in the mid-1920s when the station was modernised by the LM&SR, to access the bridge which was also used by passengers to reach the Booking Hall and forecourt. The poster on the right is advertising the popular British Railways travel guides.

Crewe North 'Jubilee' 4-6-0 No. 45629 *Straits Settlements* is subject to close examination from two young enthusiasts and their father as it waits at Platform 3 with a Down express. It had been fitted with AWS in June 1959 and this picture was probably taken shortly after that.

*Kenneth Field/Rail Archive Stephenson*

CHAPTER 10 - LLANDUDNO JUNCTION TO BANGOR

Stanier Class '3P' 2-6-2T No. 40081 shunting in the goods yard at Bangor in 1960. It was transferred there from Carnforth in June but only stayed for three months before returning to Carnforth from where it was withdrawn a year later. Bangor had a long association with the taper boiler 2-6-2Ts, from the late 1930s into the early 1960s, and they worked mainly on local passenger trains to Afon Wen and Llandudno, and freight on the Afon Wen line.
*Kenneth Field/Rail Archive Stephenson*

Two ladies sitting on an empty parcels trolley wait for an Up train as Stanier Class '4P' 2-6-4T No. 42567 stands in Platform 2 opposite. No. 42567 was transferred to Bangor from Camden in June 1960 and was there until November 1963. Then big Stanier tanks first arrived at Bangor in 1946, taking over the passenger trains on the Afon Wen line from their less powerful '3P' cousins; by mid-1952 the shed had fourteen Stanier or Fairburn 2-6-4Ts and the allocation remained at this level until the early 1960s.
*Kenneth Field/Rail Archive Stephenson*

Although the rebuilt 'Patriot' and 'Royal Scot' 4-6-0s used the same Type 2A taper boiler, they had a number of detail differences of which the most noticeable were the cabs. The 'Scots' kept their original cabs but the 'Patriots' had to have new Stanier pattern cabs because the originals were too narrow for the new firebox. The front end of the 'Scot' has two footsteps on the inside cylinder cover and the bufferbeams differ in shape and rivet type. Both No. 46163 *Civil Service Rifleman* and No. 45527 *Southport* were allocated to Holyhead, but No. 45527 only has the shed code painted on where its plate would be fixed. No. 46163 arrived in June 1960 and left two years later, while No. 45527 was there from May 1961 until June 1963, suggesting that this picture was taken at the east end of Bangor station in summer 1961. *Southport* is on the Up Platform line and *Civil Service Rifleman* is on the Up through line.

English Electric Type '4' diesel-electrics began to work on the North Wales main line in late 1959 but by 1962 their regular duties were still mainly only on the 'Irish Mail' and the 'Emerald Isle Express'. No. D231 *Sylvania* is ready to depart eastwards, probably in 1963, over Caernarvon Road bridge before entering Bangor Tunnel and has a BR four-wheel CCT at the head of the train suggesting that this is one of the regular mail trains from Holyhead.

## Bangor shed

By the end of the 1950s, all of the pre-Grouping classes had gone from Bangor and the shed is populated by Stanier, Ivatt and BR Standard designs. Those which can be identified are Class '5' No. 44683, 2-6-4T No. 42587 and Class '2' 2-6-0 No. 78059. On the right by the coaling stage, with its 70,331 gallon capacity tank above, are several Ivatt 2-6-2Ts and Class '5's; the turntable was out of picture to its right. The L&NWR northlight-roof shed, which was opened in 1884, was designed to accommodate twenty-four locomotives. The shed was coded 7B from 1935 until March 1952 when it became 6H under the Chester District; it was closed in June 1965.

An unusual allocation at the shed from January 1956 until October 1957 was L&YR '0F' 0-4-0ST No. 51221, transferred from Crewe South to shunt the coal siding. However, *The Railway Observer* reported in August 1956 that it '*was lying at the back of the shed, out of use ... apparently having been found unsuitable for this job*'. It was still at Bangor when the Manchester Locomotive Society visited on 5th May 1957 and their report noted '*well hidden so as to be invisible to the casual visitor stood the L&Y 0-4-0ST 51221. The 'Pug' looked rather forlorn despite the specially whitened stone plinth below*'. The initials of its former owner are beginning to show through the black paint. The 1901-built No. 51221 moved back to Crewe South in September 1957 and then to Bristol Barrow Road in June 1958 where it worked until withdrawal in January 1960.

# 11 – Bangor to Afon Wen

The branch from Bangor to Afon Wen left the Chester & Holyhead line at Menai Bridge and was built in two stages. The first, from Menai Bridge to Port Dinorwic and Carnarvon, was opened in 1852 by the Bangor & Carnarvon Railway and immediately leased to the Chester & Holyhead Railway before vesting in the L&NWR in 1867. The section north from Afon Wen was opened in 1867 by the Carnarvonshire Railway but did not meet the Bangor & Carnarvon, stopping short of Carnarvon at Pant which was about 1½ miles south of Carnarvon; the L&NWR took over the company in 1870. There was also a third line terminating at Carnarvon, the Carnarvon & Llanberis Railway from Llanberis which was completed by the L&NWR in 1869 after the original company ran into financial difficulties.

Finally, in 1870 the lines were linked by the Carnarvon Town line and the L&NWR had a branch from Bangor to Afon Wen, where it met the Cambrian Railways line from Portmadoc to Pwllheli and the line from Menai Bridge to Carnarvon was doubled. (An 'e' was officially added to Caernarvon by the LM&SR in 1925 but today the Welsh spelling of Caernarfon is used).

Diesel multiple units began working on the branch in 1957 when there was a winter weekday service of eight trains each way between Bangor and Afon Wen, seven working through to Pwllheli, with three more running between Bangor and Caernarvon, and a similar level continued over the next few years. The average running time over the 25 miles 61 chains was seventy-five minutes in each direction. The DMUs only operated one or two of the trains each day and most services remained in the hands of the steam 2-6-2Ts and 2-6-4Ts until 1959 when more Derby twin-set DMUs were delivered. The Afon Wen to Caernarvon section was closed under the Beeching Plan in December 1964 but the Menai Bridge-Caernarvon line was retained until January 1970. It was finally closed in February 1972, after a stay of execution following the Menai Bridge fire in May 1970 when it was reopened to handle the Holyhead Freightliner traffic which was shipped onward by road.

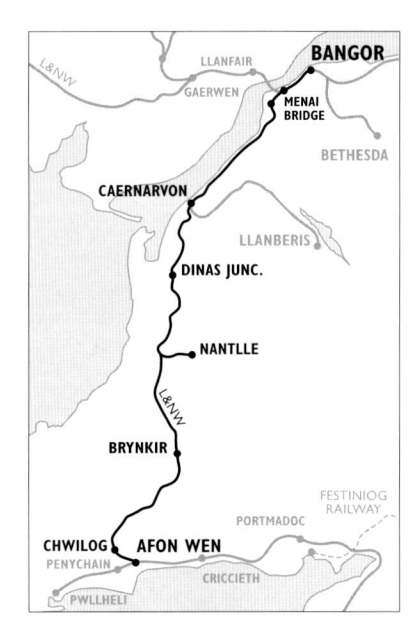

After the opening in 1947 of Butlin's Holiday Camp at Penychain, just west of Afon Wen, traffic in the summer months increased considerably since most visitors arrived by rail. On summer Saturdays until the early 1960s the line was transformed from a sleepy branch by the traffic to Butlin's of between fifteen and twenty return workings, often loading up to ten or more coaches.

**Caernarvon**

Fowler 2-6-4T No. 42366 at Caernarvon working the Stephenson Locomotive Society/Manchester Locomotive Society Caernarvonshire Rail Tour on 5th May 1957. Starting from Bangor, the tour first visited the Bethesda Branch, returning to Bangor before running down the branch through Caernarvon as far as Nantlle to visit the quarry where two horses took the party for a short ¾ mile trip in a set of steel slate tubs on the 3 ft 6 in gauge tramway. The Fowler tanks had been tried on the branch passenger services in summer 1937 but the under-powered 2-6-2Ts of both Fowler and Stanier design were used instead until 1946 when Stanier and Fairburn 2-6-4Ts took over most of the trains. In 1954 four Fowler engines, Nos 42415-42418, were transferred from Gourock in exchange for four of the Fairburn engines, but they lasted only two years and were replaced by BR Standard 2-6-4Ts in 1956/7. Soon after this picture was taken the cover over the footbridge was removed and the wooden L&NWR building on the island platform, visible on the left through the bridge, was replaced by a single storey brick structure.

CHAPTER 11 - BANGOR TO AFON WEN

There is plenty of activity on the platform as a Derby 'Lightweight' DMU stands in the Bangor bay at Caernarvon before working back to Bangor, shortly after the units were introduced on the line in 1957. The main platform, known locally as the 'Down & Up', to the right of the picture was signalled for bi-directional working and could hold up to fifteen coaches; the small wooden platform on the left was known as the 'Back Bay'. Caernarvon No. 2 signal box, a standard L&NWR design with 51 levers, is just visible through the footbridge. The steeple of Christ Church, now deconsecrated, dominates the background.
*Kenneth Field/Rail Archive Stephenson*

BR Class '4MT' 4-6-0 No. 75031 from Mold Junction at the south end of Caernarvon with a very short goods train in 1960 on the Down & Up goods line which ran to the west of the station. Freight traffic remained busy until the late 1960s with an Esso tank farm at the harbour (out of picture to the left). The footbridge to the island platform is now uncovered.
*Kenneth Field/Rail Archive Stephenson*

## Brynkir

On summer Saturdays in the 1950s the Ivatt Class '2' 2-6-2Ts regularly double-headed, either with other Class '2' tanks or with a Class '3' or Class '4' tank, on the heavily loaded special trains bound for Penychain and the Butlin's Holiday Camp. No. 41276 from Rhyl was working on one of these with a Stanier 2-6-4T at Brynkir while another 2-6-4T waits on the adjacent Up line. Usually the pairs of tanks worked bunker-to-bunker so that the leading engine faced forward after reversal at Afon Wen, but in this case they are chimney-to-chimney.

## Chwilog

BR Standard Class '3MT' 2-6-2T No. 82032 arrives at Chwilog in July 1963 with the Saturday working of 'The Welshman' to London, reporting number '1A42', hence the express passenger headlamps and headboards on the coaches. The long staff had been exchanged for the token for the single line section to Brynkir and the porter/signalman waits for the train to stop in the platform before returning his Home signal to danger. No. 82032 was in its second spell at Machynlleth, from November 1962 until July 1964 when it moved to Bangor which was its final shed. Note the station name picked out in white-washed bricks to the left of the engine.

Stanier Class '5' No. 45198 approaching Chwilog in 1964 with a paper 1K03 headcode indicating a train to the Liverpool area. Note the 'CHESTER' depot name on the bufferbeam; it was allocated there between November 1963 and October 1965. No. 45198 is paired with tender No. 9002 which was one of three prototype 4,000 gallon tenders built in 1933. This was intended for 'The Turbomotive' but delays in construction of No. 6202 resulted in the tender being used instead for No. 6100 *Royal Scot* on its tour of the United States. The three tenders were rebuilt in 1935 as nearly as possible to conform with the new standard 4,000 gallon tenders. Their original flat side sheets were replaced by curved topped sides, but they were subtly different from the standard tenders, with a different rivet pattern on the tank sides and a curved cut-out at the top of the side panelling. No. 45198 ran with the tender from 1944 until withdrawn in September 1967.

## Afon Wen

Ivatt Class '2' 2-6-2Ts Nos.41239 and 41212 depart from Afon Wen towards Caernarvon with a returning holiday special from Butlin's, probably in 1954 before No. 41212 was transferred away from Bangor in February 1955. No.41239 was there from July 1952 until August 1953, moving to Chester Northgate until June 1954 when it returned to Bangor. Both engines were built by British Railways, No. 41239 in September 1949 and No. 41212 in August 1948. The Class '2' tanks spent most of their time on the Amlwch and Bethesda branches but were regularly used on summer Saturday trains from the north. They worked bunker-to-bunker so that the leading engine was facing forwards after the trains to or from Butlin's at Penychain reversed at Afon Wen. Note the Great Western Railway lower-quadrant signals.

After the Second World War the Bangor-Afon Wen line was worked on weekdays almost exclusively by 2-6-4Ts from Bangor, supplemented by 2-6-2Ts and later Stanier Class '5' 4-6-0s on summer Saturdays. Both Fairburn and Stanier Class '4' 2-6-4Ts were used until 1954 when the former were transferred to Scotland in exchange for Fowler 2-6-4Ts. These together with some of the Stanier engines, including No. 42444, were replaced by the BR Standard version in 1956. No. 42444 which is refilling its tanks after arriving at Afon Wen was at Bangor from June 1953 until September 1956 when it moved to Bury.

Another Bangor Stanier 2-6-4T No. 42588 approaches Afon Wen station on a Pwllheli-Liverpool train composed of early LM&SR coaches, brought out of the sidings for a Saturday excursion train in the mid-1950s. The maximum load for a 2-6-4T over the steeply graded line was six coaches which led to most of the holiday trains being double-headed. Engines were usually changed at Bangor and until the late-1950s tender engines were rarely used down the branch.

Stanier Class '5' No. 45417 double-heads a Stanier 2-6-2T coming off the Caernarvon line in June 1957. The train has four ex-L&NER coaches at the front followed by a number of BR Mark 1s.

The Stanier 2-6-4T has uncoupled and waits on the former turntable road beside the twin water tanks as No. 45417, a long-standing Bangor engine from 1949 until 1963, departs tender-first towards Penychain having run around the train. Weight restrictions on the Western Region lines from Afonwen prevented the use of larger engines than the 2-6-4Ts until 1956 when the route was raised from 'Yellow' to 'Blue'. The Class '5's were then permitted to work between Afon Wen and Pwllheli 'subject to the observance of all service restrictions and providing the speed does not exceed 40 mph'

2-6-4 tank engines galore at Afon Wen on 30th June 1962. Nearest the camera is Fairburn 2-6-4T No. 42211 which had been transferred to Bangor from Birkenhead in June 1961 and was withdrawn at the end of 1962.

Afon Wen viewed from the footbridge looking west with the private road to the station on the right, also on 30th June 1962. The small hut at the end of the platform ramp housed the water pumping equipment and in front is the Down starter with a route indicator below the arm. The Butlin's Holiday Camp at Penychain is just out of picture at the top right. The train arriving from Pwllheli behind BR Standard '2MT' 2-6-0 No. 78002 will reverse here to go forward to Bangor. No. 78002 was built at Darlington in December 1952 and was allocated to Machynlleth from May 1953 until August 1963 when it was transferred to Wigan Central. The junction between the Caernarvon and Pwllheli lines was immediately after the rear coach of the train.

# 12 – Bangor to Holyhead

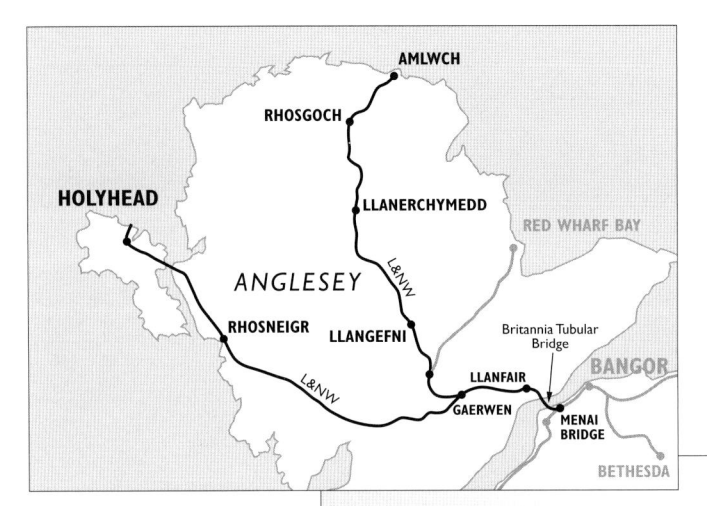

At Menai Bridge station, 1½ miles west of Bangor, the line to Caernarvon and Afon Wen branched off the Chester & Holyhead Railway which then crossed over the Menai Straits using Robert Stephenson's Britannia Tubular Bridge. The bridge, which opened in 1850, was the last part of the line to Holyhead to be completed.

Further west, the branch from Gaerwen to Amlwch was opened in 1864 as far as Llangefni and throughout in 1867. The line from Gaerwen to Holyhead was notable only for the severity of its gradients, on either side of the Cefni valley and the descent into the port of Holyhead which was reached across a causeway over the Cymyran Strait which separated Anglesey from Holy Island.

## Menai Bridge

Ivatt 2-6-2T No. 41239 at Menai Bridge with a local train from Bangor to Holyhead or Amlwch in 1956. It moved away from North Wales in 1960, spending three months at Widnes before going to Camden where it was usually employed on shed pilot duties and also on ECS work at Euston.

A passenger standing in the brick shelter on the Down branch platform watches as a BR Standard 2-6-4T arrives at Menai Bridge from Caernarvon, probably in 1957. Eight of the class had been transferred to Bangor in Autumn 1956 replacing its four Fowler 2-6-4Ts and some of the Stanier 2-6-4Ts too.

'Royal Scot' 4-6-0 No. 46140 *The King's Royal Rifle Corps* leaves Menai Bridge station with the Holyhead portion of the Down 'Welshman' on 3rd September 1957. It was originally named *Hector* which was replaced by the regimental name in 1936. The 'Welshman', which was reintroduced after the Second World War in June 1950, had portions for Portmadoc and Pwllheli which were taken off at Bangor; it was withdrawn at the end of August 1963. The Caernarvon line curves away on the right up a gradient of 1 in 128 which steepened within a short distance to 1 in 78. This picture was taken from site of the Menai Bridge No. 2 signal box which controlled movements in the freight concentration yard. The yard was a small seven-road affair with its own ground frame, the Up exit from to which is in the left foreground. Direct access from the Down direction could be made via the Caernarvon line.

*K.L. Cook/Rail Archive Stephenson*

BR Class '4MT' 4-6-0 No. 75026 takes the Caernarvon line passes through Menai Bridge station with the 'North Wales Radio Land Cruise' train on 3rd September 1957. This was the Western Region cruise train which ran on Tuesdays and Thursday starting at Pwllheli and running west through Portmadoc, Barmouth to Corwen and then up to Rhyl where it reversed and ran back along the North Wales coast and to Caernarvon and Afon Wen before terminating at Barmouth. No. 75026 had been allocated to Oswestry since the start of 1957 and was there until August 1958 when it was transferred to Chester West.

*K.L. Cook/Rail Archive Stephenson*

Menai Bridge station looking east with a BR Class '4' 2-6-4T which has just arrived with a train from Caernarvon in 1959. The narrow island platform prohibited anything other than a narrow timber shelter. Menai Bridge No. 1 signal box in the centre background controlled the junction and opposite was a small goods yard with a goods shed.
*Kenneth Field/Rail Archive Stephenson*

Stanier Class '4' 2-6-4T No. 42544 arrives at Menai Bridge with a local train from Caernarvon, with the sharp gradient immediately out of the platform visible beyond the rear coach. The Down Caernarvon platform on the left was provided with a substantial brick shelter. In the right background is the freight concentration yard which appears quite busy. No. 42544 was allocated to Bangor from June 1959 until September 1961, and this picture was probably taken in 1959. Menai Bridge station closed to passenger traffic in February 1966 and goods services in February 1968.
*Kenneth Field/Rail Archive Stephenson*

**Britannia Tubular Bridge**

As the inscription says, Robert Stephenson's Britannia Tubular Bridge was erected in 1850. He employed the same principles as he used on the Conway Tubular Bridge but the wrought-iron tubes were of more substantial cross-section and much longer at 1,500ft compared with 425ft. Fowler 2-6-4T No. 42366 pauses at the site of the former Britannia Bridge station on a Stephenson Locomotive Society/Manchester Locomotive Society Caernarvonshire Rail Tour on 5th May 1957. Participants were allowed to alight at the Caernarvonshire side of the bridge with many walking across the tops of the tubes and climbing to the tops of the towers to photograph the bridge from above. The less energetic stayed on the train which then went to Llanfair where it reversed before collecting the others on the Anglesey side on its way back and returning to them to its start point at Bangor. No. 42366 was a long way from its usual haunts, having been allocated to Stoke since October 1956.

BR Class '4' 4-6-0 No. 75014 leaves the bridge with the 2.40pm Holyhead to Euston on 3rd September 1957. Note the L&NWR cast trespass signs in both English and Welsh and one of the two pairs of limestone lions 'guarding' the bridge. They were 25ft long, 12ft high and 9ft wide, with paws 2ft 4ins across and were given Grade II listing in 1998 but unfortunately are now much less prominent due to the proximity of the road bridge built as part of the reconstruction in 1971/2.

*K.L. Cook/Rail Archive Stephenson*

A brand new Derby two-car diesel multiple unit, later Class '108', emerges from the Up portal of the Britannia Bridge in early 1959, but it is not certain that this was what had drawn a crowd of enthusiasts to the lineside. The bridge had four spans, two above the water and two on the approaches and was supported by three massive stone towers, the centre one on the Britannia Rock enabling the two main spans to be kept to a length of 460 ft each. In order to meet Admiralty requirements there was clearance of 101 ft above the high water mark.

English Electric Type '4' No. D337 leaves the Britannia tubular bridge with an Up train from Holyhead on 21st August 1966. On 23rd May 1970 the bridge caught fire with the blaze lasting nine hours as the tarred timber roof caught fire and the tubes became white hot, buckled and split. Several locomotives and DMUs were stranded on Anglesey, some being recovered by road. The DMUs provided a shuttle service on the island. The damage was so severe that it had to be completely rebuilt at a cost of over £3 million with steel spandrel arches replacing the tubes, although the three towers and the four stone lions were retained; it was eventually reopened on 30th January 1972.

*Brian Stephenson*

## Llanfair

Stanier Class '5' No. 45055 shunts an Up goods at Llanfair in 1959. The station became world famous as a result of a publicity exercise using a fifty-eight-letter name taken from two nearby villages, Llanfairpwllgwyngyllgogerychwyrndrobwllllantysiliogogogoch. The name translates as 'St. Mary's church in the hollow of the white hazel near a rapid whirlpool and the church of St. Tysilio near the red cave'. Its other claim to fame is that it was twice closed permanently and subsequently re-opened three times. The first was in 1966 followed by a re-opening with a temporary platform in May 1970 after the Menai Bridge fire closed the line into Anglesey; passengers were transported by bus to and from Bangor. When the bridge re-opened in 1972 the temporary platform was demolished. Then in 1973 the station was re-opened, financed by the local authority, as the abbreviated Llanfairpwll, the local name for the village.

*Kenneth Field/Rail Archive Stephenson*

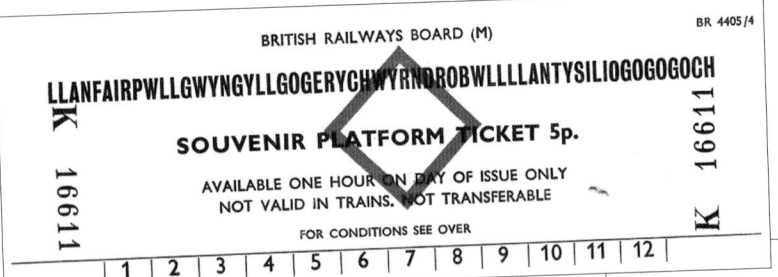

*Above*: One of the half a million six inch long cardboard tickets produced by the LMR in 1962 in an inspired piece of public relations; by the time the station was closed for the first time in February 1966 only a few thousand remained.

*Right*: Until 1956 the station had standard signs with the abbreviated name Llanfair PG together with an 80 ft long wooden sign made by a local porter. These were replaced by 20 ft long fifty-eight-letter three-part enamel nameboards. One of these two signs disappeared in 1961 only to be found the next day in the grounds of a school at Reading! The large letters on the platform shelter 'CROESO I FÔN' translate to 'Welcome to Anglesey'.

## Gaerwen

'Britannia' No. 70046 rushes through Gaerwen in the late afternoon sun with an Up parcels train in the mid-1950s. It was allocated to Holyhead from new in July 1954 and remained unnamed until September 1959 when it became *Anzac*. Gaerwen became a junction station in 1865 after the Anglesey Central Railway's passenger service to Llangefni began.

Two photographers have captured BR Caprotti Class '5' No. 73128 at Gaerwen with a Down express in the early 1960s. It was at Patricroft from August 1958 until February 1964 and the again from April 1964 until withdrawal in May 1968. The signal box on the left is Gaerwen No. 1 which had 20 levers and survives today; Gaerwen No. 2 which was in the 'V' of the junction closed in December 1966.

## The Amlwch Branch

The Anglesey Central Railway's 18¾ mile long branch from a junction at the west end of Gaerwen station on the Chester & Holyhead Railway to the port of Amlwch on the northern coast of Anglesey was completed in June 1867 and was worked by L&NWR locomotives and stock. The L&NWR took over the company in 1876 and in 1909 built a 6¾ mile line from Holland Arms, 2¼ miles from Gaerwen, to Red Wharf Bay but this proved uneconomic and its passenger service ended in 1930, and the line was closed completely in 1950. Bangor shed supplied the motive power for the Amlwch line which until 1948 had been worked by L&NWR 2-4-2Ts and 0-6-0s, but these were replaced by new Ivatt Class '2' 2-6-2Ts in early 1949. Two-car Derby 'Lightweight' DMUs took over the passenger services in May 1956, although the first non-steam operation was by the ACV three-car diesel railbus prototype for a few weeks in mid-1953. In 1954 a private railway was built from the branch just outside Amlwch station to the Associated Octel chemical works sidings which remained in use after the withdrawal of the branch passenger service in December 1964.

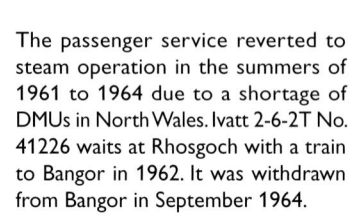

The passenger service reverted to steam operation in the summers of 1961 to 1964 due to a shortage of DMUs in North Wales. Ivatt 2-6-2T No. 41226 waits at Rhosgoch with a train to Bangor in 1962. It was withdrawn from Bangor in September 1964.

No. 41226 arrives at Llanerchymedd with a train from Amlwch on 26th July 1963. The trains were allowed around forty minutes for the journey between Amlwch and Gaerwen, times varying by a couple of minutes for some services. The single platform at Llanerchymedd was in a rock cutting and hence there was insufficient space for a crossing loop.

CHAPTER 12 - BANGOR TO HOLYHEAD

Ivatt Class '2' 2-6-2T No. 41239 at Amlwch during one of the two spells it had at Bangor; in 1952/53 and from June 1954 until July 1960. Engines on the branch usually worked bunker-first from Bangor, as prescribed by local operating instructions, but No. 41239 is facing in the other direction.

The Amlwch branch was the stamping ground of Bangor's allocation of Ivatt tanks. No. 41233 prepares to take a train back to Bangor in the mid-1950s. It went there from new in 1949 and stayed until June 1965, except for a few months at Rhyl in early 1955.

Bangor's 2-6-2Ts worked the daily passenger and goods trips on the Amlwch Branch which ran to the northern coast of Anglesey. They replaced the ex-L&NWR tanks in 1947 and were used until May 1956 when DMUs took over. There was a temporary reversion to steam operation, mostly during the summer months, from the end of 1961 until the services ended in 1964. This picture was probably taken in mid-1962 after 41226 was transferred to Bangor from Birkenhead in April of that year.

## Holyhead

One of the three Class '3F' 0-6-0Ts at Holyhead in the 1950s, No. 47476 stands beside Holyhead signal box in 1960. It was built by Vulcan Foundry in 1927 and had moved from Warrington to Holyhead in 1945; it was there until withdrawal in May 1964. The four-bay signal box with a 100-lever frame was a LM&SR Type '11C' dating from 1937 and is still in use today.
*Kenneth Field/Rail Archive Stephenson*

Moving to the other side of the signal box the shed was built at a higher level than the main line which dropped down at 1 in 76 on the approach to the station platforms. In view are BR Class '5' No. 73073, a Stanier Class '5' and a 'Royal Scot' which are representative of its allocation from the mid-1950s until the early 1960s. No. 73073 arrived in February 1960 and was there until February 1963 when it moved to Llandudno Junction. The shed closed to steam in December 1966 and remained in use as a diesel depot until demolished in 1991; the site is still in use as part of Holyhead TMD. Note on the right the letter 'H' in bricks which was the start of the word Holyhead on the embankment.
*Kenneth Field/Rail Archive Stephenson*

'Britannia' No. 70048 is ready to depart from Platform 2 at Holyhead with the 'Irish Mail' in the mid-1950s before it was named *The Territorial Army 1908-1958* during 1958. It was a regular on the Irish mails until the end of 1959 when along with Nos 70045 to 70047 and 70049 it was transferred away from Holyhead and replaced by new English Electric Type '4' diesel-electrics.

The TSS *Princess Maud* was a familiar site on the Holyhead to Dún Laoghaire route for almost twenty years until September 1965. It was built in 1934 for the LM&SR and was originally used on the Larne to Stranraer route. *Princess Maud* served as a troop ship during the Second World War, and was reconditioned after the war, moving to Holyhead. It was used as a spare and relief vessel, running Holyhead-Dún Laoghaire extra sailings in summer, then worked as relief on other Irish Sea routes when the regular vessels were being overhauled. The integration of the station with the ferry terminal in the late 19th century L&NWR modernisation is apparent.

*Kenneth Field/Rail Archive Stephenson*

A father and son look at Stanier Class '5' No. 44935 as it waits to leave Holyhead with an Up express. This picture was taken during the three months it was allocated to Holyhead, between June and September 1959. Note the large amount of litter which has blown onto the track in Platform 2. The goods yard on the right became a Freightliner terminal until the traffic finished in March 1991.
*Kenneth Field/Rail Archive Stephenson*

Probably on the same day, a very unkempt 'Jubilee' No. 45674 *Duncan* waits to leave Holyhead with an express for Crewe. It was at Crewe North from December 1941 until March 1963.
*Kenneth Field/Rail Archive Stephenson*

'Royal Scot' No. 46151 *The Royal Horse Guardsman* waits to leave Holyhead with an Up express. It was allocated to Crewe North from June 1958 until July 1959 when it moved to Longsight and had been fitted with AWS in June 1959 which narrows down the date of this picture to just four weeks in June/July 1959. The building on the left is the Station Hotel, opened in 1880 as part of the London & North Western Railway's development of the port. It was at the point of the new 'V'-shaped inner harbour and the arrival platform was on its left and the departure platform on the right; both had overall roofs. The introduction of sleeping accommodation and dining facilities on the motor mail vessels *Cambria* and *Hibernia* in 1948, led to the hotel's closure in 1951. It was used as railway offices until the 1970s, later dealing with Sealink ferry tickets, and was demolished in 1979. The offices of Stena Line, which now operates the ferry service to Dublin, occupy the site. On the right is a '3F' 0-6-0T by the small goods shed for local freight with the large shed for the Irish traffic visible to the right.

*Kenneth Field/Rail Archive Stephenson*

A decade or so later, the Class '40' diesel-electrics had taken over the express work and there are several more changes behind No. 314. The end panel of the overall roof has been opened up in the centre, the goods shed demolished and a Freightliner terminal constructed. The terminal was opened in 1970 on a large site on the west side of the inner harbour and had ten full length sidings and a large travelling gantry crane. Up to four trains ran each day providing services to Birmingham Lawley Street, Manchester Trafford Park and to Willesden and Ripple Lane in London. The terminal was closed in March 1991 after the services became unprofitable and the area was redeveloped to provide parking for the ferry service.